From Suffering to Triumph

Richard Wurmbrand is a Hebrew Christian and a Romanian evangelical pastor. He and his wife Sabina suffered great persecution under Fascism and Communism. Under the Communist authorities in Romania Richard Wurmbrand spent fourteen years in prison for his faith. He and Sabina were ultimately rescued by the Norwegian Israeli Mission and the Hebrew Christian Alliance.

After coming to the West the Wurmbrands were used by God to set up the international Christian Mission to the Communist World, which now has bases in many different countries.

In 1990, after the revolution in Romania which overthrew Ceaushescu's dictatorship, Richard and Sabina were able to return to their homeland from which they had been banned for twenty-five years. This book is not so much about the suffering they found there as about the beauty which God gave to the Romanian believers during their years of oppression.

Other books by Richard Wurmbrand:

Tortured for Christ
In God's Underground
Sermons in Solitary Confinement
If Prison Walls Could Speak
Alone with God
Christ on the Jewish Road
Marx—Prophet of Darkness
Answer to Moscow's Bible
Little Notes Which Like Each Other
100 Prison Meditations
From the Lips of Children
My Correspondence with Jesus

RICHARD WURMBRAND

FROM
SUFFERING
· TO ·
TRIUMPH!

**The dramatic
and extraordinary sequel
to *Tortured for Christ***

kregel
PUBLICATIONS

Grand Rapids, MI 49501

From Suffering to Triumph by Richard Wurmbrand.
© 1991 by Richard Wurmbrand and published in
1993 by Kregel Publications, a division of Kregel, Inc.,
P.O. Box 2607, Grand Rapids, MI 49501. All rights
reserved.

Cover Illustration: Vic Mitchell
Cover & Book Design: Alan G. Hartman

Library of Congress Cataloging-in-Publication Data

Wurmbrand, Richard.
  [From torture to triumph]
  From suffering to triumph / Richard Wurmbrand.
      p.   c.m.
  Orginally published: From torture to triumph.
Eastbourne: Monarch, 1991.
  Sequel to: Tortured for Christ.
      1. Wurmbrand, Richard. 2. Luthern Church—
Romania—Clergy—Biography. 3. Persecution—
Romania—History—20th century. 4. Romania—
Church history. 5. Romania—History—Revolution,
1989. 6. Romania—History—1989. 7. Romania—
Description and travel—1978. 8. Communism and
Christianity—Romania. I. Title
BX8080.W86A3   274.98   1993   92-42091
                                            CIP

ISBN 0-8254-4061-0

   1 2 3 4 5 Printing / Year 97 96 95 94 93

Printed in the United States of America

Introduction

A brother who had been terribly tortured by the Communist police shared the same prison cell with me and told the following incident:

> I once saw an impressive scene in a circus. A sharpshooter set out to demonstrate his skill. In the arena was his wife, with a burning candle on her head. From a distance he shot the candle so that it fell, leaving his wife unharmed.
>
> Later I asked her, "Were you afraid?" She replied, "Why should I be? He aimed at the candle, not at me."
>
> I thought about this when I was under torture. Why should I be afraid of the torturers? They don't beat me. They beat my body. My "me," my real being, is Christ. I was seated with Him in the heavenly places. This—my real person—could not be touched by them.

I have lived through the years of enforced exile with the image of such heroes of faith in my heart. Now, on my return to my homeland, I again found this same spirit among the Christians I met.

My purpose in writing this book is to help you ascend to such heights.

A Prophet in Disguise

After eight years in Romanian Communist jails, I was released, but only for a short period. I had failed to pass the test. The Communists considered my sermons after liberation as bad as those before my arrest. The brainwashing to which I had been subjected in prison had not been effective. My mind still harbored the same "wrong" religious ideas. There was only one solution: send me back to jail— this time for twenty-five years, though I eventually served only six. My total prison experience was fourteen years.

Captain Stanciu of the *Securitate* (Romanian Secret Police), who had to interrogate me when I was arrested for the second time, was an apostate Christian who had been brought up in the home of devout believers. Now he jailed God's children to convince them that they were wrong. For some unknown reason, he was nice to me. At the risk of losing his own liberty if overheard, he whispered to me on the first day, "My superiors have committed a terrible mistake in ordering your arrest. At first you were an unknown pastor in a small church. Then we imprisoned you for eight years and turned you into a national figure. Now all Romanian Christians know you, and you have become a hero in their eyes.

"Your rearrest will make you an international figure. That was the wrong thing to do."

7

Though an enemy of the gospel, he uttered a prophecy, just like Caiaphas the high priest who sentenced Jesus to death (John 11:50).

When I was freed in 1964 after my stint of fourteen years in Communist dungeons, I was not allowed even to attend churches. Pastors of congregations where I tried to worship were threatened by the Communists: "Don't allow Wurmbrand to enter your building—or else!" I had no other choice but to leave the country, which I did with my wife Sabina and my son Mihai in December 1965.

For twenty-five years we have been forced exiles during which time the Romanian Communists have not ceased to denounce me in their press as their archenemy, principally because of my books exposing their activities and my involvement in the Christian Mission to the Communist World. God used me to start this mission devoted to spreading the gospel in countries under atheist dictatorships and to helping the persecuted. I was able to write books that have been translated into over sixty languages. For more than two decades I have traveled and preached the world over in the service of this mission, which has expanded to all continents. I have indeed become internationally known. Captain Stanciu's prophecy has been fulfilled.

Return to Romania

I value the fellowship of brothers and sisters of all nations and confessions, but my heart has never ceased to yearn for my Romanian fatherland, the country in which I had been born twice.

Patriotism is not very fashionable today. But since Jesus taught us to love even our enemies, how can we do so if we don't love our own country first? And so wherever I traveled, the heart that beat in my breast was the bleeding heart of my country and the oppressed Romanian church. There seemed to be no hope of my ever seeing it again, except in heaven where the great reunion will take place. Although we felt no hope for this earth, my wife and I practiced hope against hope and saw it fulfilled. In a matter of a few days God overthrew Ceaushescu's bloody dictatorship. He and his wife were killed. I could finally return to my beloved country.

My lovely wife Sabina and I boarded the plane in Zurich. We were not sure if we would be allowed to enter the country. A few days before our departure, the Romanian King Michael I and Queen Anna had tried to return. Though much loved by the people, who of course were not consulted, they had been denied entry by the Communists. They had been stopped at Zurich airport. The new Romanian government, presumed to be democratic, forbade the King and Queen, pride of the Romanian nation, to visit their own land in which the Communists were intruders as puppets of the Soviet Union. (In January 1991, the Romanian government finally restored their citizenship.) The new government, with Iliescu as President, still consists almost entirely of Communists—"reformed" Communists to be sure, but still Communists. A tamed wolf is still a wolf.

A stewardess interrupted our reveries: "Will passenger Richard Wurmbrand please identify himself?" My heart sank. We thought we were sure to be asked to leave the plane.

To our great surprise and relief, unknown friends who had heard that we would be on this jet had sent us a box of chocolates and a beautiful message of encouragement.

Some two hours later we heard the almost unbelievable words: "Please fasten your seatbelts and prepare to land in Bucharest."

My granddaughter Amely once gave this explanation of the city's name: "Romania is a Communist country. If they catch you there with a Christian BOOK, ARREST follows."

This explanation was no longer valid when we arrived in Romania, exactly a quarter of a century after we had left. The mission to which I belong, and many others, now cross the border with truckloads of Christian literature. Our organization has even created a large printing press in Bucharest itself where we hope very soon to produce Bibles and other books. The printing presses themselves would have cost us a fortune which we did not have. But the printing press of Germany's ruling Communist Party went broke, and their machines were sold at auction. We obtained first-class machinery for half the price. Moreover, Romanian Bibles will be printed on machines that had printed atheist literature!

We are also setting up the first Christian bookshop and video store.

Seeing Angels and Jesus

At long last we were in Romania! Overcome by emotion, I kissed the soil.

Later, when I returned to western Europe and America, many people asked me about the situation in Romania. I cannot really comment on the situation in its totality. I can say only what I saw. The observer is part of the reality observed. Beauty is in the eye of the beholder. If one has a good eye (Matt. 6:22), a dove's eye (Song 1:15), he will see things differently from the one who looks with other eyes.

When Peter and John heard a rumor that Jesus had risen, they immediately ran to the tomb, entered, and saw linen and a handkerchief, nothing else. Then they left (John 20:7). Moments later, Mary Magdalene looked into the same tomb and saw two angels. How come the disciples didn't see them? But Mary Magdalene was not satisfied with seeing angels. She thought to herself "Where there are angels, there must be something even better." She did no more than turn her head, but she saw the risen One.

I went to Romania to see angels and Jesus. They are my first love. Why should I spend time with lesser beings? I saw angelic beings and Jesus dwelling in the lives of His saints.

Only One Sadness—Not to Be a Saint

Twenty-five years had passed since we left Romania. A voice whispered in our ears, "Why not give up hope? Perhaps no one will remember you."

We could hardly have anticipated the crowds that gathered from many cities far and near to welcome us. Our joy and astonishment knew no bounds. The first person I saw was my former cell-mate Nicolaie Moldovanu from the Army of the Lord, a Romanian version of the Salvation Army, but without uniforms and bands. We had been in the same cell in the ancient prison in Gherla. The regime had been very harsh. From time to time, wardens would shout, "Everyone on the ground!" It was winter. We had no sweaters, let alone overcoats. The floor was cold concrete with not even a bit of straw for warmth.

Prisoners cursed the brutality of the wardens. Not so Moldovanu. He believed that praising God was better than cursing Communists. With a beautiful smile on his lips, he would say, "Let's forget our surroundings. I'll sing you the song I just composed while lying on my stomach." It was a hymn full of joy, hope and praise, sung now in many countries.

I remember the Orthodox priest Ghiush with whom I had been in the Jilava jail near Bucharest. The whole prison is underground. Cows graze over the subterranean cells.

I was then in the eighth year of my sentence, I had grown used to everything. But one day a whole group of newcomers, all Orthodox priests, were brought in. From time to time, the wardens would shout, "All priests out in the corridor!" and would beat them.

I sat down near the priest Ghiush, whom I had known when we were both still free. My intention was to comfort him. "Are you sad?" I asked. He lifted beautiful eyes to me and replied, "I know only one sadness: not to be a saint."

Moldovanu was the same type of man. What an honor it was for me to receive his brotherly kiss! I did not feel worthy to untie his shoelaces.

Holy Kisses

Many were the kisses I received at the airport. I believe that kisses should have a much greater place in Christ's church. Paul wrote, "Greet one another with a holy kiss" (Rom. 16:16), not with a cold handshake. Jesus Himself longs for our kisses.

"Kiss the Son" wrote the psalmist (Ps. 2:12). He is not satisfied with anything less.

One evening Jesus was at the house of a Pharisee named Simon who had invited Him to dinner. Doubtless, on the table were beautiful flowers, choice foods, and wine. Jesus looked at them and said with sadness, "I have come into your house, and you did not give me a kiss." This was what He really desired.

In the New Testament, the word for worship in the original Greek is *proskuneo*, which means a reverential kiss. When Jesus was on earth, it was easy to kiss Him. His mother Mary must have kissed Him countless times. But how can we kiss Him now? My wife had more kisses from me when I was in jail than she has now. So often when I want to kiss her now, the phone rings or I have to hurry to a meeting. But kissing is not so much a touch between two pairs of lips as a coming together of two loving hearts.

Unsinged by Fire

And so I was kissed by Constantin Caraman who had been one of the main contacts of our mission with the underground churches. It was through him that we had channeled much relief to the families of those who were being persecuted.

He, too, had been in prison three times. He had worked as a slave laborer, just like my wife, building a canal uniting the Danube with the Black Sea. What a place of cruelty that had been! A prisoner was caught stealing twenty onions which he intended to share with others to enable them to swallow the tasteless food: oats cooked in water, without salt, without fat. The guard gave the prisoner a choice: twenty-five lashes on the soles of his feet or eating the onions without salt or bread. He chose the latter. Tears streamed from his eyes which swelled and made him look like a frog. In the end, he fell into convulsions.

Another time, a convoy of women prisoners were being driven from their barracks to their place of work. On the way, they saw a dog's corpse. One woman smashed its head with a stone, then others jumped on it to eat its brain, so great was the hunger for protein.

In the USSR horses were used ● carry wagon loads of stone. Prisoners picked worms from their excrement and washed them. Again, valuable protein.

I looked at the shining face of Caraman, former slave laborer. He had a triumphant, loving smile on his lips. Observing him, one would never guess what he had passed through.

In ancient Babylon, three Jewish youths who had been thrown into a fiery furnace because they refused to bow down to an idol emerged without even the smell of fire on them. So it was with Caraman and a host of other former prisoners I met.

A Convicted Pickpocket

There was Brother X. I would not have recognized him after twenty-five years, but he reminded me who he was: a former pickpocket with whom I had been in jail. He had been won for Christ when I preached in a cell full of common prisoners about Jesus' love for thieves.

Far from loathing them, Jesus went so far as to compare Himself with a thief who comes at night when the residents of the house would not expect him. Even more, He uses thieves as models for honest men. He praised thieves in His Sermon on the Mount for being good to each other.

Now we laughed as we remembered the time I fell asleep in my cell with my shoes on, only to awaken as he tried to take them off! At the time, I was moved by his kindness, thinking his desire was to enable me to sleep better. On the contrary! He had played dice, and my shoes were the stake. After winning, he expressed surprise that I failed to recognize him as their legitimate owner.

There was Vasile Rascol whom I had known from childhood. He, too, had been in jail for the crime of distributing smuggled Bibles. Now he is working with us in establishing a press where Bibles and other books can be freely printed.

My Children in Romania

I could not begin to describe everyone I knew in the crowd, but I must say at least a few words about my children.

All my friends in the West know that I have one son, Mihai. He was the only one about whom I spoke and wrote because he had emigrated with us. But he is not my only son. In the airport, Sandu was waiting. Since he had remained in Romania, I could never mention him as I didn't want to endanger him.

Many years ago I buried a Christian who had two small children. Since his widow was very poor, I took one child into my home, and he never left. He became Mihai's brother. Because he was adopted, the Communists would not allow him to leave with us. Today he is married, and I was able to meet him, his wife Sylvia, and their children.

I could embrace my granddaughter Doina whom I had never seen. She is married and has given me my first great-grandchild. I also embraced my grandson Richard, named after me. Richard had been arrested in the final days of the Ceaushescu regime and expected to be shot. In his cell he thought, "Well, I belong to the Wurmbrand family. Prison and persecution are its fate." When he was taken out of his cell for what he thought would be execution, he received an incredible surprise.

"Ceaushescu has been shot," he was told. "You can go home."

There was also Lenutza. Once, as I sat in my office, a girl of thirteen entered. She was shy, poorly dressed, and very thin and pale.

"Are you Pastor Wurmbrand?" she asked.

"Yes."

"Then you are my father from now on. My own father is an alcoholic and has forsaken us. My mother is always bringing home some other man who beats and chases me. I heard that you are a good man, so I will be your daughter."

I called my wife from the kitchen. "Congratulations! You have given birth to a child without any birth pangs. Here she is."

She, too, remained in our home. Just after I was kidnapped by the Communists in 1948, my wife, instead of brooding about her misfortune, prepared a beautiful wedding for Lenutza.

She, too, was at the airport, with her husband Gheorghe and their daughter Cornelia.

We had six other children, all war orphans whom we had taken for our own, though under Communism it was not possible to adopt them legally. There was plenty of joy and noise in our two-bedroom apartment. We never had to go to the circus or cinema for amusement. We had plenty at home.

All six of these children were killed on one day. To reveal the circumstances would mean accusing some whom I would not like to mention. Great sorrow has been my companion from childhood. God has taught me to rejoice in tribulation. He is with me in the free world too. My wife and I suffer here more than we ever suffered under the Nazis and Communists.

The Politics of Kindly Smiles

At the airport we all joined in singing, accompanied by Moldovanu on the harmonica. I'm sure the angels participated in this joyous reunion. Police officers from the *Securitate* (the dreaded Communist organ of repression) stood by. They are still in power and wear the same uniforms, but they have been paralyzed by the uprising of December 1989 which overthrew their boss Ceaushescu.

After the singing, there were speeches. A videotape was made by brothers Neureder and Wieser of our German mission, great friends of Romania who had come especially for this occasion. A number of individuals from the crowd went with us for an intimate meeting in a house on University Square. From the window we could see the many thousands who demonstrated against the government day and night.

The University Square had been declared a non-Communist zone that refused to acknowledge the authorities. There were tents for some twenty hunger-strikers (one in the 36th day) who were calling for the demise of the government. Some of the demonstrators, almost all young, sang a hymn, "Better to be a rascal and a scoundrel than a Communist." This hymn was in response to the prime minister who had characterized them in such terms. From a balcony, leaders of the opposition harangued the Communists.

The aversion to Communism was understandable, but it was not wise to turn it into a political platform. The Communist Party had four million members. Together with the membership of the Communist youth and their nearest relatives, they numbered ten million, the great majority of the voters in a country of only twenty million. Instead of trying to win the rank-and-file Communists to their side, the leaders of the opposition frightened them. The Communists thought, "We will all have to suffer if the opposition comes to power." Unwise anti-Communism assured the success of the Communists in the elections.

Jesus knows best what is right in the political sphere. Words of love for the enemy serve the cause better than expressions of hate. It would have been easy to win the hearts of Communists. They were shattered by the bankruptcy of their ideology in the Eastern European nations. They were depressed as well as disappointed. With a few good words, President Sadat of Egypt obtained great concessions from Israel, after five bitter wars had led to terrible loss of lives and territories for the Arabs.

I am for the politics of kind words and friendly smiles in all human relations.

The Hebrew word for "to tell" is *lesaper*, which comes from *saper*, meaning sapphire. "To tell" in Hebrew means "to give a jewel."

We should only speak if we have a jewel to give. If you can enrich another, if you have a jewel to give, talk. If not, it is better to keep your mouth shut. If this simple Hebrew rule were respected, there would be no family strife, no divorce, no political splits, no feuds in churches or between individuals.

Subverting Communism with the Gospel

The Communists have done great evil in Romania, but most of them were unaware of it. They did not know about the satanic roots of Communism, which I have revealed in my book *Marx—Prophet of Darkness* (Marshall Pickering). Many only joined the Party for a better job or higher education. They should have found compassion, but instead they were hardened by evil attitudes.

Finally, the Communist President Iliescu had had enough of the demonstrators in University Square. One day he shot and wounded many of them. Over a thousand were arrested on one day.

How is it that Communism has crumbled, that, while it is far from losing the war (China, Cuba, North Korea, Vietnam—about one-fifth of mankind—are still under Communist one-party rule), it has lost some decisive battles?

For years politicians believed that Communism could only be defeated through nuclear deterrents. They spent billions and billions of dollars producing them and now have to spend billions more in dismantling them as useless. Others believed we should accept Communism as an unchangeable reality and come to terms with it. Their slogan was *détente*.

The Romanian dictator Ceaushescu was a maverick. Like Tito, he had played the game of being a

Communist apart, at odds with Moscow, but friendly with the West. He was even granted a title at the British court. But he was a Communist just like the other dictators, only of a different stripe. There are several species of tyrants just as there are several species of wolves, but they all have the same primary characteristics.

Neither anti-Communist armaments nor courting the Communists helped.

In all my writings and speeches I advocated something else: "Communism infiltrates and subverts the free world. Let us subvert the Communist world with the gospel. Let us win them with love. Christ taught us to hate sin but love the sinner. Let us introduce, by secret means if necessary, the word of God. Let us raise an army of prayer warriors."

Alliance with Angels

Furthermore, I said, we should ponder the secret of the Jewish people. Though small in number, they have had to fight powerful foes in order to exist. In the end, they have conquered all their enemies. Today Israel faces the enmity of hundreds of millions of Arabs who will succeed no more than the powerful Romans, the Inquisition, or the Nazis.

The Jews are 3% of the population of the United States. They are 25% of its millionaires, but also of its revolutionaries. They play an enormous role in science and the arts. A large percentage of Nobel prize-winners are Jewish. The nation of Israel, although among the smallest, is in the headlines every day. A third of the world now awakens from the nightmare in which a Jew—Marx—played the principal role. The only one who can save it from this nightmare is another Jew—Jesus.

What is the secret of the uniqueness of the Jewish nation? One can say God willed it, and that is true. But there was one event in Jewish history through which this will was manifested.

Jacob, ancestor of my people (I am Jewish), fought with an angel and prevailed (Gen. 32:28). With one man on its side, a colony of ants is invincible in its fight against other ants. With a few steps the man can destroy the enemy. Likewise one man, one nation, one church with an angel on its side will prove in the end invincible.

Each of us has a guardian angel. How can two walk together if they do not agree (Amos 3:3)? It was one of the greatest events of my life to know my guardian angel. Many Christians worked together with their angels for the defeat of Communism. Learn from them and do the same! In some places angels are described as having wings. They are necessary for communication between men and a distant God. But if God is nearer, wings are not needed. In Jacob's vision, it was enough that angels had a ladder (Gen. 28:12). For some, even a ladder is not needed. The angel of the Lord surrounds them (Ps. 34:7). He is at their disposal.

Christian Mission to the Communist World and other similar organizations that followed its example have worked hard in the spiritual as well as practical realms. Angels were by our side. Our prayers were added to the prayers and sacrifices of numberless martyrs. And so it happened that Communist walls have come tumbling down.

How the Revolution Began

A Romanian bishop, one of the many who became stooges of the Communists, fired the Reformed Pastor Tökes of Timisoara for preaching faithfully. When he was to be evicted from his home and church, a crowd of Christians of all denominations and several nationalities surrounded his house and obstructed the police. The number of demonstrators grew. When they proceeded to march toward the center of town, the army was called out to stop them. The soldiers began shooting, and many were killed or wounded. Little children gathered on the steps of the cathedral and sang religious hymns. Again the troops fired, and some children died. The rest sought shelter in the cathedral, but heartless priests had locked the sanctuary.

Then an amazing thing happened. The entire crowd, instead of fighting the army, knelt and prayed. This was too much for the soldiers. They refused to shoot any more. Meanwhile, the whole town had gathered. Pastor Dugulescu seized the opportunity to address everyone from the balcony of the Opera House. A poem by Constantin Ioanid, "God Exists," was recited. The crowd shouted, "God exists!" Leaflets with the text had been distributed. Some who knew the music began to sing the song that had been composed for the words. Soon thousands joined in singing it again and again. It became the song of the revolution.

One day when my son Mihai, at about age five, was walking with us through the park, he stopped in front of a man sitting on a bench reading.

"What are you reading?" he asked with childish simplicity.

"A novel."

"Better read the Bible," said Mihai, "because if you don't follow it, you will go to hell."

"What kind of words are those?" asked the stranger.

"Do you see the tall man with a little lady there behind me? They are my parents. Ask them and they will tell you everything. It's a very serious matter."

Curious by now, the man did ask. It turned out he had been a member of a virulent anti-Jewish organization. Through the witness of a little Jewish boy named Mihai, he was converted and became one of the best Christian poets of Romania. It was his song that became the hymn of the revolution.

When it became known elsewhere that innocent people had been killed in Timisoara (it was rumored they numbered thousands), other demonstrations broke out spontaneously in different locations. Thirteen children, the oldest fourteen, made a barrier with their bodies against the troops of the Secret Police who could advance only by murdering them. The children knelt and shouted, "Please don't kill us!" The police paid no attention. When the first fell, the others did not run away but remained kneeling with arms outstretched in love and childish confidence toward the murderers as they continued to beg, "Please don't kill us!"

A cross now stands where the children died.

A legend arose in Romania. It said that angels began the revolution. Coming down from heaven, they entered the children, giving them holy courage like that of the good angels who had defeated the hosts of Satan in heaven. The martyrdom of these children gave victory to the unarmed against an army. Tanks and troops were called out against the populace, but in vain. The soldiers were as fed up with the dictator as the people. In Sibiu, two Orthodox priests who were lifted onto tanks asked everyone to kneel for prayer. The demonstrators, numbering thousands, as well as soldiers and officers, did so. An "Our Father" was said together by those who still remembered prayers. Soldiers and citizens embraced. It was no longer possible to repress the uprising.

Communists Hate Each Other

At the same time, another scenario was taking place in the capital.

Communists have a religion of hate. They hate not only capitalists, Christians, and Jews, but also each other. Almost all members of the Central Committee of the Communist Party of the USSR had been killed by their comrade Stalin. In China, the president of the Communist republic, Liu-Shao-Chi, died under torture ordered by his comrade Mao-Tse-Tung. In Romania, Lucretiu Patrashcanu, the Communist who brought his party to power, was killed by his own secret police.

So it happened that Ceaushescu's comrades in evil deeds, Iliescu, Roman, and others, plotted to overthrow him. For them the uprising in provincial towns was the spark they needed. They prepared to arrest Ceaushescu who had just returned from Iran and was scheduled to deliver a speech from a balcony in the center of Bucharest.

When he spoke, instead of receiving the usual cheers (which were compulsory), Iliescu's men in the secret police began to boo. No one else would have dared. But this signal was enough to stir up the crowd. They had long desired to boo. Nothing could stop them now. The shouts against Ceausescu became louder and louder. Sensing the danger, he fled, but something was wrong with his car. He flagged down another. The security officer who was with him and his wife drew out a revolver and instructed the driver— who happened to be a Christian—where to go.

Pretending that the battery was low, he stopped right where men were ready to apprehend their leader. After being paraded on television, Ceausescu and his wife Elena were killed. Several of his adherents were jailed. Romania now has a new government, but one which consists (at the time of writing) almost exclusively of former Communist leaders, schooled in Marxism from youth. They claim to have renounced Communism, but Communism does not abandon a Communist.

The Bible tells the story of the exodus of the Jews from slavery. They followed Moses for a while, but at the first opportunity they made a golden calf to bow down and worship, just as they had seen the Egyptians do. They had gone out of Egypt, but Egypt had not gone out of them. The idolatrous practices learned while they were slaves in a heathen country remained in the Jewish mind for centuries.

The new government of Romania, like the old, has also shot and jailed innocents. Ceausescu can be happy about his successor.

A Church I Founded

On Sunday, I had my first service in the Baptist church of Valaori Street in Bucharest.

In a sense, I was its founder. The Communists were not the first to persecute evangelicals in Romania. By 1940, the right-wing Iron Guard, who were fanatically Orthodox, had come to power. The first thing they did was to forbid Baptist, Adventist, Pentecostal, and Brethren Churches to worship. Consequently, all their buildings were closed. Then Marshal Antonescu dispensed with the Iron Guard and established his own dictatorship, again banning religious freedom. Not one Romanian-language evangelical church remained open. Hundreds of evangelical Christians were sentenced for up to twenty years. The Orthodox Church stood solidly behind this persecution. There has been no Reformation in Romania. The Orthodox Church is still as authoritarian as the Catholic Church was before Vatican 2.

All Lutheran churches were free except mine because I was Jewish and so were the majority of my congregation (the government was fiercely anti-Jewish). The Lutheran bishop Städel was not inclined to defend us. He gained renown through his sermon that proclaimed, "Mankind has had three geniuses: Christ, Beethoven and Hitler. I dare to assert that Christ is even greater than Hitler."

And so, like the Baptists and other evangelicals, we, too, gathered in the underground.

Toward the end of the war, a friend of ours, the Swedish ambassador van Reuterswärde, succeeded in obtaining the authorization for us to worship. In one day, we removed all the furniture from our apartment and turned it into a church. As soon as this was known, hundreds of brethren from all the forbidden denominations came to our services which we had to conduct five times a day. Thus we were the only Romanian-speaking evangelical church.

When the Nazis lost the war, my former church again enjoyed religious freedom and was given back its old building. Those who had gathered in our apartment formed a Baptist congregation. This has become the Valaori church. Thus, in a sense, its Baptist pastor Talosh is my successor.

Many who now gathered to hear me had known me personally before. The others knew about me, my books, and my life story. For them I was not a mere human but the incarnation of a legend that had grown more and more beautiful over the years, to the point of losing touch with reality. I had the problem of convincing them that I was not the legendary hero they imagined, but an ordinary man.

The Wurmbrand Land

A joke is told in Romania: the dictator Ceaushescu's car was forced to stop on a country road for a small repair. Nearby he saw an old peasant woman painfully shoveling dirt and asked about her life. She told him how hard it was and then asked, "Who are you?"

Amazed at not being recognized, he replied, "Read the newspaper. Watch TV. They tell who I am. I am 'the genial leader,' 'the lay god,' 'the genius of the Carpathians.' I am the one who brings truth, light and love to this country."

The woman, full of joy, shouted to her husband who was working at a distance, "Come quickly, John! Brother Wurmbrand has arrived!"

An American Christian has written a book about

Romania which he calls *The Wurmbrand Land*. Dispelling the legend, and speaking as a simple man, I preached in church after church, my heart overflowing with love and joy.

How Much Am I?

One evening I was in the Popa-Rusu church, where I had been secretly ordained as deacon during Nazi times, when it was inconceivable that a Jew should be given office in a church. But this was a German-speaking church, and the Romanian Fascists did not dare to close it.

The ordination took place in the greatest secrecy. Only the two who laid hands on me and two witnesses were present. The door was locked. The German brethren Fleischer and Strobel were not concerned about the anti-Jewish tempest raging outside.

It was in this same church that I later performed my first baptism—of a Jew who did not know one word of Romanian. During the services he would read his Russian New Testament and just let me talk. Before baptizing him I said, "I cannot just perform this ceremony. I bear a responsibility. I must find out what you have learned from Scripture. Read any verse you like and explain it to me."

He opened his Bible at 2 Corinthians 12:11 where Paul writes, "I am nothing," closed the book, and asked, "If Paul was nothing, how much are you?"

I thanked him. He knew Scripture better than I.

A Heroine of the Faith

After Bucharest, I traveled from town to town. We saw the miracles of socialism everywhere.

Where there had once been cars and trucks, men now rode behind horses. The shop windows were empty. People stood in line for hours for tomatoes, cabbage, milk. There were ration cards for many articles. An individual was allotted one kilogram of meat every two months. The streets and houses were poorly lighted.

In every town I met the great and little heroes of faith, as well as cowards and outright traitors. One heroine who traveled with us to some places was Dr. Margareta Pescaru.

In 1950, I was close to death in the prison hospital of Tirgul Ocna. The Communists had inherited from the capitalists they despised the notion that every jail should have an infirmary and a physician. However, physicians were told, "You must practice veterinary medicine on these prisoners. Give them the sort of medicine and care you would give to oxen and horses in order that they might be able to work as slaves. If they can no longer recuperate, let them die."

In such prisons we knew two kinds of physicians. Some of them, among whom were young female doctors, would be present at the torture sessions and would joke with the savages. From time to time the doctor would take one's pulse and say, "Now let him rest for a while." During this time, he—or more likely she—would amuse herself with the police officer, then say, "Now you can start again, but be careful not to beat him in the region of the heart. He might die too soon, and you won't get any more information out of him."

But there were others who took seriously their primary duty to save fife. Preeminent among them was Margareta Pescaru. A Christian, she smuggled medicine into the jail. Physicians, just like others, were frisked when they entered, but she succeeded time and time again. Many lives, including mine, were saved in this manner.

If a doctor was caught smuggling, he or she would be badly beaten, then imprisoned for many years. The risk was considerable.

Dr. Pescaru made contact with my family and friends. She also provided me, and others through me, with streptomycin, the miracle medicine for tuberculosis which was widespread in prison.

Preventing an Orgy of Cruelty

But she did even more than that. In the prisons of Piteshti, Suceava, and the Canal, the Communists had begun the so-called "reeducation" of prisoners. Some had been corrupted through promises of freedom if they would beat and torture their fellow inmates to get them to reveal deeds against the state they had not divulged during the investigation. The prisoners also had to abjure all their convictions, political or religious, for which they had been sentenced. They had to promise full allegiance to Communism.

Any method that would produce results was permitted: severe beating on the soles of the feet and on the genitals; breaking teeth with gravel; forcing prisoners to ingest feces and urine; sleep deprivation; forbidding them to go to the toilet; and any other degrading measures.

Men had to be reduced to heaps of fear, nothing else. The Communists succeeded with most of them. When prisoners were forced to run up and down the stairs pursued by whips and sticks, everyone ran for his life, which, though wretched, was at that time all that mattered to him. Some did not yield, but they were few. Some died under torture. The henchmen, not satisfied with mere killing, would urinate over the corpses.

Each prisoner was allowed to take one cup of water from the tap each day, but he first had to present it to the re-educator, who would spit in it. Then the prisoner could drink. Jesus used spittle for healing. I know one prisoner who at that time asked himself, "If Jesus' spittle could heal a blind man, can the spittle of such wicked men also heal if we accept it with quiet resignation and love for the evildoer?"

The authorities brought some of these re-educators to my prison hospital, designated for tuberculosis patients, to start their work of destruction. Re-education had been hell for the sane; what havoc would it wreak among the sick, many of them near to death? In a whisper, we communicated the danger to Dr. Margareta Pescaru. She did the unthinkable. She decided to go to the worst of beasts to plead the cause of lambs.

After traveling a whole night to the capital, she went to the top officials who had oversight of the prisons—in simpler terms, to the chief butchers. God gave her grace in their eyes, as He did to Esther in the eyes of Ahasuerus. We have no idea what convinced them. Was it her physical beauty, or rather rays of God's power shining through her? But she pleaded with success. She appealed to pride. Tirgul Ocna was the only large prison hospital; the prestige of the country was at stake, and so on. The fact is that, for the first time in the history of Romanian Communism, the torturing of innocents was stopped.

Christian Becomes
Communist Police Officer

Another hero was X. (It is not safe to reveal his name even now, since the *Securitate*, the Communist Secret Police, is still in power.) During those dark years, some wore the prisoner's garb for Christ. But X brought a greater sacrifice. To destroy the church from the inside, the Communists infiltrated their numbers, placing men who had become priests and pastors for this purpose in positions of trust. Brother X thought, "Why not reverse the process?" David said, "There is none like the sword of Goliath" (1 Sam. 21:9). Translators often believe they are wiser than the original authors and should correct them. This is true of Bible translators as well. In the original Greek in Matthew 10:1, it is written that Jesus gave his twelve disciples the power *of* unclean spirits. The English says "over," which is something entirely different.

In time of war, the enemy's spying cannot be counteracted only by preaching the gospel. There must also be counterespionage. So young Brother X became an officer of the Secret Police to serve the underground church, and especially me. Brothers and sisters who had become prisoners wore a uniform that was highly honored by believers. X was loathed as a traitor who had passed to the ranks of the enemy. Believers might well have thought, "Who knows what he really does? Perhaps he has even become a torturer."

He bore the shame and did his job well. He was not the only one. Through men such as him we came to know beforehand about threats of arrest. I was informed even after I had been exiled to the West about threats to my life.

I met this hero of the faith, Brother X. Romanian believers still don't know his story. What a privilege it was to embrace him!

Some brethren, instructed by their faithful pastors, accepted the role of becoming informers of the Secret Police when it was proposed to them (and it was proposed to almost all Christians). Police officers would meet with these "informers" in conspiratorial apartments, and we were thus able to learn the addresses. Then members of the underground church could spy on these apartments belonging to the police and learn the identity of the real traitors. These sham informers were very careful to tell the police only things that would lead them astray. It is wise to say little more, even today.

Collaborators of the Communists

I met with top leaders of different denominations. Some of them had been collaborators with the Communists. Feeling terribly guilty, they did not dare to lift up their eyes. They trembled for fear that the archives of the Secret Police and the Ministry of Cults would be opened, and the public would know all the details of what they had done. Some of them were elderly men. Considering the fact that Communism had reigned in Romania for forty-five years, they probably asked themselves what they would do at such an age, deprived of their positions and probably of their pensions as well. I tried to ease their conscience by telling them, first of all, that a measure of collaboration had been legitimate.

I was not saying that it would be right to submit

to dictators, for Paul said in Romans 13:1: "Let
every soul be subject to the governing authorities,
for there is no authority except from God." A God-
hating government is not from God. If it were, God
would be like the Jewish king Saul, who asked an
enemy, an Amalekite, to kill him (2 Sam. 1:9). God
would be advocating a kind of suicide.

I believe, with Saint Augustine, that "without justice, states are nothing more than robber-gangs."
Our duty is to uproot them as gangs and try to save
the souls of individuals in the gang.

Why, then, did Paul not write like Augustine?

I believe it is wise to say a few pleasant words to
tyrants under whom you are obliged to live, as long
as you cannot overthrow them. Daniel the prophet
said some very pleasant things to King
Nebuchadnezzar who was the Hitler of his day.
Diplomatic talk belongs in the arsenal of Christians.

Commenting on the king's dream that foretold
terrible sufferings for him, Daniel said to
Nebuchadnezzar, who not long before had thrown
Daniel's three friends into the fire. "My lord, may
the dream concern those who hate you, and its interpretation concern your enemies!" (Dan. 4:19). In his
heart, Daniel might have thought, "All the punish-
ments from God, O king, are only just, and I hope
God will not change his mind."

What Should We Render to Caesar?

Jesus said, "Render to Caesar what is Caesar's,"
a very clear teaching. The Jews were to render to the
Roman emperor what was his. Now, what was legit-
imately his in Palestine? Simply—nothing. The
Roman army had invaded Palestine by force and

ruled in a tyrannical way. The historian Flavius
Josephus wrote that, when the Jews rose up claiming
minimal human rights, the Romans crucified so
many of them "that there remained no wood for more
crosses and no place to put them." The Caesars had
planted not one tree and built not one house in
Palestine. "Give to Caesar what is Caesar's" means
give him nothing, except a boot in the back.

Who are the governing authorities everywhere?
They are the successful rebels of yesterday or their
successors. Cromwell and others fought against
tyrants in Britain; therefore the democratic regime
was God-willed. One royal house has been overthrown through violence by another; therefore the
actual queen of Britain is a God-willed authority.

Americans broke an oath of allegiance to the king
of England and made a successful revolution. The
American authorities of today are therefore of God.

The conclusion? Overthrow Communist and
other dictators. If you do not succeed, you are a
rebel. If you are victorious, you will be a ruler
appointed by God Who gave you victory.

Under Hitler, Mussolini, Stalin, Ceaushescu, as
with many despots of old, Christians have been mis-
led, by a false interpretation of this one verse from
Romans 13, to become collaborators in evil deeds.
They have failed to observe that these polite words,
"Let every soul be subject to governing authorities,"
appear only towards the end of a book that teaches
on all preceding pages that one should withstand and
tear down injustice and tyranny. This is what
Moses, Gideon, Barak, Samson, David and others
did, all of whom are honored as heroes in the Holy
Book.

I did not consider the collaborators with the Communists personally guilty. One born in a heathen or animist environment naturally becomes heathen. He cannot be blamed. Likewise one brought up in a church in which everyone submits to rogues, considers the practice normal.

One of the top leaders of the official Soviet Baptist Church, now deceased, said, "We have to be submissive to the authorities, which does not mean only to the government, but also to the KGB (the murderous Soviet Secret Police), because it is also an authority and as such is willed by God." This means that if they asked me to spy on my brethren in the faith, to report on and denounce them, knowing murderous arrests will follow, I must do so. How can one ask Christians educated in such a faith to act otherwise? It is like wondering why a child educated in English does not converse in Arabic.

I managed to have fellowship with the former collaborators who had caused much harm to individuals and churches. They had considered it right to inform the authorities about everything that happened in the church—every word spoken, every decision taken. As for the consequences of what they did? They thought, "Let the chips fall where they may."

I tried to show them understanding. I told them that for the Jews the Talmudic teaching is: when a persecutor of religion arises, the rabbis have to divide into two parties. One must stick to the inherited faith and not change even the Jewish manner of tying shoelaces. The other, on the contrary, must be friendly to the oppressor, wine and dine with him, in order to obtain at least some alleviation of suffering. The merit before God of the suffering first group is not greater than that of the second group who feast with the tyrant, provided they are prompted by good intentions. These words helped some to understand themselves better.

Some collaborated very wisely. By giving only a little verbal allegiance to Ceausescu, they were able to receive many concessions. They would abstain totally from the deification of Ceausescu who was called "the lay god," "the genius of the Carpathians," "the greatest thinker ever," and so forth. The Lutheran bishop Muller consented to be a member of the Communist parliament, though he never voted. But the little compromise of being there without ever flattering the Communist rulers had the result that the Lutheran church was among those that suffered the least.

The Traitors

The church in Romania had others besides collaborators in its ranks. Some were outright traitors who sold the lives of innocents for money, though they never got more than a pittance, like Judas with his thirty pieces of silver. Even then, I am reminded that Jesus sat at the table with Judas even after he had betrayed Him. All the many words of love spoken by Jesus to the disciples at the last meal included him, too.

Jesus said, "Let not your hearts be troubled. You believe in God, believe also in me." This was meant for Judas, who was assured that in the Father's house there are many mansions, even one for a disciple who already had the price of betrayal in his pocket, if only he would repent. Jesus was saying, "There is still time to return" as He continued, "I will receive you to myself" (John 14:1-3). When Judas led the soldiers to arrest Jesus and gave Him a treacherous kiss, Jesus even then called him "friend," for His friendship is everlasting.

In the original, John 5:2 reads: "By the sheep there was a pool" (the word "gate" here is an interpolation of the translators). Near every sheep of Christ there is an opportunity to be washed from every sin. The great tragedy is that some of the traitors were recruited not only from among the worst Christians but sometimes from the best, even from those who had been heroes of faith, who had suffered torture and imprisonment for many years. There is a Latin saying: *De hic historia silet*— "about these history is silent." Not everything should be told. Some things are too sad.

Preaching to Unseen Audiences

What were the highlights of our trip to Romania?

Sabina and I stood before the gorgeous palace of Ceaushescu which dwarfs Buckingham Palace. It is said that even the taps in the bathroom are gold, but "the lay god" never once had the pleasure of using them. The palace is built over the spot on which the Uranus prison of the *Securitate* had stood. This prison was torn down to make way for the dictator's residence. I sat in that underground fortress. I even dare to assert that I ruled from my cell, though this may sound like boasting. Let me explain.

I was kept alone in a cell from which I never saw sun, moon, stars, birds, flowers, trees, or butterflies. In time I forgot that nature exists, even that colors exist. In my dull gray world of dingy cement walls, tattered clothing, and ashen skin, I forgot what blue, green, and violet look like. There was never a book nor a scrap of paper. In that deep subterranean prison, silence reigned. I heard never a word nor a whisper. This was sensory deprivation at its cruelest.

Every night in my dark cell I preached to an unseen audience. I was accustomed to this audience, even when I was free. In 1 Peter 1:12, it says that angels desire to look into the preaching of the gospel. Whenever I preached in churches, I was aware that angels were also present, not only men. (Where else would our guardian angels be when we are in church?) I always endeavored to say a kind word for them, too. But I made the mistake of thinking that only angels could be my unseen audience. It was not so.

After I came to the West, I published three books of sermons I had delivered in my solitary cell: *Sermons in Solitary Confinement, If Prison Walls Could Speak*, and *Alone with God*.

And then something very strange took place.

I received a letter from a man in Canada who wrote that he was from a good Christian family but had gone astray as a young man and wound up in jail. There he misbehaved and was put in a solitary punishment cell. In despair, he thought how sad his godly parents must be. He would have liked to return to God but did not know how. He prayed, "God, if there is somewhere in this world another lonely prisoner who knows You, bring me his thoughts." Then he heard an inner voice telling him, "God seeks you more assiduously than you seek Him. The desire of a cow to be sucked is greater than that of a calf to suck. He seeks you and He knows how to find what He seeks. Sit quietly and confidently. He will reach you."

And then, evening after evening, he heard a kind of sermon from far away.

He repented. Mercifully, his prison term was short, and he was released. Years passed during which he married, had a family, and became a deacon in a church.

One day he entered a Christian bookshop and saw a strange title on a book cover: *Sermons in Solitary Confinement*. Having been in solitary confinement himself he wondered, "To whom does someone in solitary confinement preach?" He read the book and later wrote to me: "Mr. Wurmbrand, you did not preach to nobody. I was in solitary at the same time as you. I recognized the sermons. It was yours that I heard and that brought me back to Christ. Thank you for having delivered them."

I might not have paid too much attention to this letter if I had not received another from a lady in England who described the same sort of effect.

Then I met a French pastor. He told me he had been an unbeliever when he saw a vision of a pastor with a clerical collar who told him about Christ. He was converted and in time became a clergyman who won many souls to his Master. One day he too saw the same book, *Sermons in Solitary Confinement*. On the cover of the French edition is a picture of me wearing a clerical collar. He recognized me immediately as the man he had seen in his vision.

Preaching beyond Space and Time

The Hebrews have three words for soul: *nephesh*, *ruach* and *neshamah*. *Neshamah* is its highest stage. *The Kabbalah*, principal book of Jewish mysticism, calls it "the supersoul."

At its highest level, the soul is beyond space and time. A man enclosed behind four walls can reach men thousands of miles away. When I received these letters, they shed new light on some strange assertions of St. Paul: "The word of the truth of the gospel, which has come to you, *as it has also in all the world*" (Col. 1:5-6, my italics); "Your faith is spoken of *throughout the whole world*" (Rom. 1:8, my italics), and so on. These words seem such gross exaggerations that they could almost be called outright lies. Paul had no knowledge of Japan or America. The gospel was far from having reached even the known world. But the hidden man of the heart, the inner man, the *neshamah*, communicates beyond all boundaries. Things happen to the inner man of which the outward man, the conscious, knows nothing.

It is written that all the Jews who passed through the Red Sea at their exodus from Egypt "were baptized" (1 Cor. 10:2). They numbered perhaps two or three million. Not one knew that this was happening to them. "All those who were baptized into Christ Jesus were baptized into his death" (Rom. 6:3). Ninety percent of those baptized, even at maturity, did not know this. My wife and I learned this only years later and wondered about it. Who of us knew that we were "buried with him" (v. 4), or that our old man had been "crucified with him" (v. 6). A man would remember if he had been crucified. None of us does. Things happen with our *neshamah*, things which the conscious, that very little part of our mind, does not experience.

Personally, I never had the experience of accepting Christ as a novelty. When, at the age of twenty-seven, I heard the gospel from a village carpenter, I had rather the impression of recognizing something I had always desired, for which I had been searching. Plato wrote, "To know is to recognize."

A real sermon that flows from the inner castle of the heart, a sermon to which the preacher also listens in wonder, never having thought that he knew such things, is an existential event remembered by listeners even after decades. It reaches to the ends of the earth and produces an impalpable effect. In his book, *The Peace Child*, Richardson tells about many missionaries who have found tribes with a knowledge of tenets of the Christian faith that they had no way of learning from other Christians. Sermons from far away have reached them.

As my wife and I stood before Ceaushescu's enormous palace, I remembered these things and meditated on them. In my subterranean cell I had more joy than he could ever have dreamed of, even when he was at the peak of his power. His work was in vain. In this palace, as in all others, one day there will not remain one stone on another. But souls won for Christ will remain for ever and ever and will ascend without end from glory to glory.

Sabina and I embraced each other and said a prayer of thanksgiving.

Winning Souls in Jail

From there we went to the former building of the Central Committee of the Communist Party. From its balcony, Ceaushescu had started to deliver his last speech when he was rudely interrupted with shouts of "Murderer! Criminal! Down with

Communism!" He fled in a helicopter that was on the roof and went to his death. This building is the former headquarters of the Secret Police and hosted another underground prison. There, too, I spent two years in solitude. Deep underground I had preached the gospel by tapping on the wall to prisoners in cells on either side. The inmates changed frequently.

The Norwegian pastor Fjeldstad, a missionary in Israel, told me he had met there a Jew who, when he started to tell him the gospel, replied with a smile, "You come too late. I heard the gospel years ago from a fellow inmate who tapped in Morse code when I was in a solitary cell in Romania. I believed it then and I still believe it."

I rejoiced every step I took in Romania. Each place brought back beautiful memories.

We stood before the actual police headquarters where my wife and I had often been detained in Fascist and Communist times. In Bucharest, I saw again a sister who, with her father, a Baptist preacher, had been imprisoned by the Fascists in these police headquarters, along with me and several others. We had been denounced for organizing underground services in homes. We remembered how happily we had sung there.

Then there was the Malmezon prison in Bucharest, where I had been in both Fascist and Communist times (it was much worse under the latter). During the war, six brothers and sisters were there. It was a loose arrangement, with male and female prisoners together during the day. On one occasion the commander, a colonel, entered the room and shouted, "I heard that you sing your hymns here, which is forbidden. What kind of hymns are these? Let me hear one."

We sang "O sacred head, now wounded, with grief and shame bowed down." He turned around and left without saying a word. Many years later I heard from Filip Shmuilovici, an outstanding Hebrew Christian who had been my fellow prisoner on this occasion and now lives in Israel, that the colonel had become a brother in Christ. Our singing might have helped others to salvation as well.

The Central Place of My Life

I found myself again on Olteni Street, where my church had been. On the same street there had also been an Orthodox church and a synagogue. Ceaushescu had no need of such buildings so they were all torn down. Olteni! What memories I had of this place. It was here, through many tears, that I had said my first public prayer of repentance. The service had been conducted by Pastor Adeney of the Anglican Church's Mission to the Jews. He had dedicated his life to the Jews and had preached some forty years with little visible fruit. But he did not abandon his mission. It became evident later that he had not worked in vain. He had brought to Christ Isac Feinstein, who became a well-known Hebrew Christian preacher and died a martyr's death. Another was Asher Pitaru, who was with me later in a Communist jail. Prisoners and Communist wardens alike called him "Mr. 1 Corinthians 13," because this was his main subject when speaking to anyone, even to the guards, who treated him respectfully. When Pitaru was before court, an intimate Christian friend of his was the main prosecution witness against him. He never spoke about this man with anything but love; he never mentioned his sin. These and many others were the fruit of Adeney's service.

The main preacher was Pastor Ellison, himself also of Jewish descent. Olteni was the place of my conversion and later my pastorate. Everyone called the church "the church of love" because, though nominally Lutheran, it was really the only interdenominational place in Romania. Worshipers of all kinds—Orthodox, Baptists, Pentecostals, Nazarenes, Adventists—felt at home in this nest. When someone who believed in christening brought his child, we all rejoiced with him. When another asked for baptism at maturity, those who baptized children were present to celebrate. My colleague, Pastor Solheim, preached his belief that at Holy Communion we receive with bread and wine the real body and blood of Christ. I said that I believe in a symbolic presence. No one quarreled about it. Jesus had said, "Take, eat, drink." He had not said, "Squabble about which interpretation is correct." Communion is what it is, not what we think about it.

We took good care of the poor in this church and helped many other churches as well. It was here that we started the first secret mission to the Soviet army that had invaded our country. New Testaments and Gospels were printed for them.

The Olteni church is dear to my heart for another reason: it was here that we met secretly in the attic, which was my "parsonage," the Rev. Stuart Harris, now Chairman of the International Christian Mission to the Communist World, and his friend the Rev. Moseley from the USA. They were the first foreign visitors who did not allow themselves to be fooled by official church leaders. We met at night, and I told them the whole story of our suffering.

This meeting was really the foundation stone of our Mission to the Communist World, which has expanded to over forty countries, has introduced millions of Bibles, New Testaments, Gospels and other pieces of literature into Communist lands, and has mobilized hundreds of thousands in prayer for the persecuted. We also helped with radio broadcasts and financial support for families of prisoners.

Are You Ready to Enter a Chariot of Fire?

I delivered many sermons in Romania which I cannot reproduce here. But I would like to share a few of my main thoughts connected with the special situation in that country.

I spoke about the ease with which one can be raptured to heaven. Anyone can be raptured today if he is willing to travel as Elijah did. This is how: "A chariot of fire appeared with horses of fire . . . and Elijah went up by a whirlwind into heaven" (2 Kings 2:11).

"Is anyone here ready to enter such an uncomfortable chariot?" I asked. "Then he can be raptured at once.

"Where would you like to be taken? Jesus has given us a great promise: 'To take him who overcomes I will grant to sit with me on my throne, as I also overcame and sat down with my Father on his throne' (Rev. 3:21).

"Anyone can come to sit on this throne. Daniel gives us a description: 'His throne was a fiery flame, its wheels a burning fire. A fiery stream issues from it' (Dan. 7:9). Are you ready to sit on such a throne? Then you can have a place of honor on it.

"I come from the West where some preach easy salvation. Just believe, that is all. If you believe, you will not only have heaven in eternity but also health and prosperity here.

"You might escape totally from Communist persecution, but this false western teaching is around the corner to destroy your spiritual life much more than Communism could have done.

"To be a Christian means to believe in Him, which is to believe in His sacrifice on Golgotha and His teaching that we too must deny ourselves and follow Him. We are meant to be crucified and buried together with Him, not in a physical sense (though in southern Sudan Christians have been crucified even in 1990) but in fighting to the uttermost against sin, the world and the devil, and never giving up even if you lose many battles. About Britain, it is said that in war it loses all the battles but has the final victory. So must we too.

"Christian faith can bring healing. My wife, my son, and I have been healed repeatedly by faith. But it is also true that many fall sick because of their faith. Perfectly sane men became Christians. For this they were jailed, beaten, tortured; they lost their health because of Christ. He has made many prosper in business, but many with a good living lost everything. Their houses and property were confiscated, or they had to pay heavy fines again and again because they became Christians.

"Don't serve Christ for what you can get from Him. John and Mary Magdalene and others loved

Christ when He could do nothing for them. He hung in pain and thirst on a rude cross and even shouted words that seemed to indicate despair.

"Mary Magdalene loved Jesus, period. Even if He could give nothing. She loved Him even when He was a corpse in a tomb, and she spent money on spices to embalm Him.

"Where, then, is Christian joy? Paul says, 'I now rejoice in my sufferings for you.' A Christian weeps with all those who weep—not only for those who weep for a little while, but also for those who weep and gnash their teeth in hopeless pain in eternity. Not only Jesus, but also all His disciples share in everyone's pain.

"They fill up in their flesh what is lacking in the afflictions of Christ. He was not satisfied with just being crucified for mankind. He descended into hell. Even if no one did Him any harm there, just being in such a place of horror, hearing the shrieks and the howling, sensing the fire and brimstone, must have been terrible. No sensitive man can read Dante's description of hell without shuddering.

Union with God

"But this was not enough for Jesus. By His choice He is crucified again as often as spiritual Christians fall away in sin (Heb. 6:6).

"This, too, is not enough for Him to reveal the abundance of His love toward us. He inhabits believers. He lives our life with us. He does it patiently, but He still sometimes asks, 'How long will I bear with you?' (Matt. 17:17). Every fall, every sin, every weakness and doubt of ours tortures Him, because He has become one with us. In us, He is not a separate 'I.' A symbiosis has taken place.

"In Hebrew, Isaiah 48:12 sounds like this: *Ani-Hu-Ani rishon, af ani acharon.* Translated literally: 'A me who is a me-he is the first; one who is only me is the last.' God and I have united in one person. There is no grief of mine He does not share, no doubt, no rebellion, no mistake. It is also His. Out of love, He takes it upon Himself.

"And we find our joy in the supreme priestly service of bringing ourselves as sacrifices. We suffer for everyone, for Christ the sufferer lives in us. Christ is not only in glory now, but has also remained the Man of Sorrows acquainted with grief."

I gave an extreme example of this taken from life.

"Baptize Me or I'll Shoot You!"

Annmarie had been arrested for her underground work in the church. As is usually the case, she was beaten and tortured to make her betray the names of other brethren and sisters implicated in her work. The temptation to yield did not even occur to her. She was so preoccupied, I would say possessed, by one thought: how to bring salvation to the torturer. For her the question was not how to escape further pain, how to forego being sentenced to long years of prison, but how to make her torturer escape sin and hell.

She said to him, "You beat me in vain. You will never beat out of me my love, not only for God, but also for you."

The torturer laughed heartily. "What a foolish girl you are! I beat you, and you declare your love for me."

There were times when one could have lengthy

talks with the torturers. Occasionally, they got tired of beating.

One of them said to me, "You prisoners shout when you are beaten. Why? You feel pain, but what is your suffering compared with mine? You get beaten at most for half an hour. We have to beat so many. There is not time for more than that. Then you rest in your cell. But I have to beat eight hours a day. I have done this six days a week, twelve months a year, for ten years. The only music I hear is the noise of the whip and the cries of the tortured. It is maddening.

"In the evening I get drunk and then go home, where I beat my wife, too. This is my life. I am a greater sufferer than you."

Torturers took coffee breaks. They would also smoke cigarettes. If the prisoner smoked, they would offer him a cigarette as well. For a quarter of an hour, the torturer would be a jolly fellow, ready to converse and even joke with his victim.

And so this one torturer took the girl's declaration of love as a joke.

She continued: "I will now tell you words that under normal circumstances you would never hear from a girl. While you beat me, I looked at your hands. How beautiful they are! I imagine how your wife enjoys it when you caress her. I put to you a simple question: is caressing not better than beating? When you caress your wife, you and she have pleasure. You surely cannot enjoy torturing more than caressing.

"You have very attractive lips. How your wife must have rejoiced when you first kissed her. Is kissing not better than swearing at people and cursing with foul words?"

He gave her a slap. "Stop this stupid talk! I am not interested in your idiotic lies. You'd better tell us with whom you worked in your underground activity. We are not in the business of love here, but in discovering counter-revolutionist activities."

She responded, "I have a boyfriend who not only loves me. He simply is love itself. From Him I have learned to love everyone heartily. I love those who do me good. I love those who hurt me."

He gave her a blow, and she fell to the concrete floor of the cell, hitting her temple, and fainted.

When she awoke, she saw the torturer sitting, deep in meditation. He asked her, "Who is this strange boyfriend of yours who taught you to love both the good and the bad without distinction?"

She told him, "It is Jesus," and spoke to the torturer about him.

"How can I become His friend too?" he asked.

"You must repent of your sins, put your faith in His dying for you on the cross, and be baptized."

"Then baptize me," he demanded.

She replied, "I cannot baptize you," which was not true. Anyone can baptize in such exceptional circumstances. But she did not know this.

He took out his revolver, pointed it at her, and said, "Baptize me or I'll shoot you!"

If this seems strange, it shouldn't. He fulfilled the words of Jesus, who said, "Some take the kingdom of God by violence" (Matt. 11:12). "By violence" can mean threatening with a revolver.

He dragged her to a pool, threw her into the water, and she baptized him. It was a sincere conversion. The proof was that, at great risk to himself, he succeeded in freeing her.

This Annmarie is an *Ani-Hu-Ani*, a symbiosis between Him and herself. Even under the worst of tortures, she had one thought: the salvation of the worst of men. She accepted an especially severe beating because of her missionary endeavor, but she also triumphed.

Forgiving a Torturer

Continuing my sermon, I insisted: "You have all suffered much at the hands of the Communists, in one way or another, physically or psychologically or socially.

"There is something lacking in the cross of Christ. All He did for mankind till now is not enough. You belong to His body, you are a new embodiment of His. Wherever you are, Christ is, as it was when the Virgin Mary was pregnant. If she went from the kitchen to the dining room, He was with her. He and His mother were one. You are part of His body, just as He was part of Mary's body.

"Take all tribulations upon yourself with resignation and joy. They are Jesus' tribulations first. Thus you will fill up what is lacking in the cross of Christ. Apply this to all the hurts you receive in the family, in your job, in society.

"The Uniate priest Demeter had been a prison colleague of mine. When he was in jail, a warden amused himself by beating him again and again with a hammer on the backbone. As a result, Demeter was paralyzed and has lain unable to move for twenty years.

"Now there has been a revolution, and Ceaushescu has been overthrown. The *Securitate* officer who had destroyed his life came to

Demeter's door and said, 'I know I cannot be forgiven. What I did was too heinous. But only listen to my words of apology and I will go.'

"The priest replied, 'For twenty years I have prayed for you daily. I waited for you. You are forgiven.'

"This is the essence of Christianity. Any other attitude is not.

"When Jesus taught us the 'Our Father,' to make sure we understood the most important part of it He added immediately, "If you forgive men their trespasses, your heavenly Father will also forgive you. But if you do not forgive men their trespasses, neither will your Father forgive your trespasses' (Matt. 6.14-15)."

Communists Broadcast My Sermons on Television

Something very strange happened after I had delivered a few sermons in which I stressed our duty to love our enemies, including the Communists. My sermons were broadcast at state expense on TV.

For years the Communists had kept me in solitary confinement so that I could not tell my thoughts, considered poisonous, to even one fellow-prisoner. Now the Romanian government, still Communist, took special care to ensure that the whole populace heard what I had to say.

Why?

The government well knows that the people hate its activities. The dictator Iliescu, wiser than his predecessor Ceaushescu, understands this. He considered it profitable for the oppressed to be taught to love their oppressors. The paradox was that my enemies and Christ's were eager for people to listen to me. In fact, today Communist leaders actually beg Romanian pastors, "Please preach all you want, even in public squares, but stress love for one's enemies. Otherwise the people will tear us to pieces."

Did Jesus foresee that His teaching of love to the uttermost would be welcomed by His enemies when they were in danger and would help the spread of the gospel because it offered them protection?

We dare to walk our dangerous way, in which we seem to be fellow-travelers with the worst of men and to strengthen their hands (this is the case with almost all who do good to those who do evil), because we believe that the Word is God and in the end this Word will change the hearts even of God-haters.

Two thousand years ago, the Jews hated their Roman oppressors. Was it because Jesus taught love for one's enemies that Pontius Pilate, Roman governor of Israel, desired to free Him?

Love, just because it is love, exposes itself to all risks—even the risk of being misused by the wicked—in order to win all. We will not give up teaching love for one's enemies, even though for a time God-haters profit at our expense.

Not Interested in My Sermons

We met Angela Cazacu.

She had been our coworker during the War, busy stealing Jewish children from the ghettoes and thus saving lives, smuggling food and clothing to scores of female Christian prisoners in the Mislea jail, and so on. Then the Soviet army invaded our country. She gave out Russian Gospels and New Testaments in railway stations to trains full of

Soviet soldiers. Some sisters were arrested for this, but started again as soon as they were released.

When I was in the Tirgul-Ocna jail in 1951, Romania had its heaviest snowfall ever, in some places five feet high. At the time I was seriously ill with pulmonary and spinal tuberculosis, as well as a couple of other illnesses. When the cold was most bitter, the prison commander gave the order that no prisoner was allowed to have more than one blanket. We shuddered endlessly with the cold. Transport was at a standstill. The administration had no food to give us. No family members or friends could come to the jail with a parcel because of the snow. Only one prisoner of the hundreds who were in this jail received a parcel at that time. Angela, whose name in Romanian means "female angel," made her way to the jail through the mountains of snow and left a package for me. At that time I looked like a skeleton. I accepted the gifts that she had struggled to bring us, and we shared them, comforted that we were not alone.

Now she attended a service at which I preached. I asked her what she thought about the sermon. Her reply was not very complimentary: "I did not listen to it much. I was not very much interested in what you said. For me it is enough to see that, after all you have endured, you are well enough to preach. I see your radiant face. I feel the love that emanates from you both. If you had given only the blessing at the end of the service after someone else had preached, it would have been enough for me."

Do Today What You Neglected Before

Many leaders from the World Council of Churches, Lutherans, Baptists, Reformed,

Pentecostals, Adventists, World Federations, and world-renowned evangelists now flock to Romania and the other freed Communist countries. None of them has apologized for having praised non-existent religious liberty in Romania under Communist rule. None has apologized that during the forty-five years of terror not one of these great bodies or any national denomination had done anything to give practical help to the families of Christian martyrs. Though my name was known abroad, my children never received one cent, one parcel, or one letter expressing concern during all my years of imprisonment. I could vouch for the fact that not one of the families of Christian prisoners of that time received anything until our Christian Mission to the Communist World was formed.

That is all in the past now, and I would not mention it if this hard-hearted attitude was not still present. I challenge anyone to ask the leaders of these denominations if they have in their budget at least £50 ($100) a year for families of Christians jailed in Muslim countries. There are prisoners of faith in Egypt, Malaysia, and Iran. Christians are heavily persecuted in Muslim Turkey. Perhaps the universal church could make up now for what it neglected then. There are missions that now work effectively in this regard in Communist countries. Let the denominations do the same in Muslim countries.

The Language of Passion

When I started to tell in the West the story of persecution in the East, I was accused at the very least of gross exaggeration. Bishops and leading evangelists who had been to Russia, Romania, and

Hungary were quick to give the Communist rulers certificates of good behavior. I myself heard one of the most renowned evangelists in the USA say upon his return from Russia, "There is more religious freedom there than in Britain." Such kind words were also spoken about my homeland.

Did I exaggerate?

First of all, what's wrong with exaggeration? Why should anyone object to it, since it is the normal response of individuals speaking about a subject that they feel passionately about?

We read in Mark 1:4, "*All the land* of Judea and those from Jerusalem went out to John the Baptist and *were all baptized* by him." Is this an exaggeration or not? Those who place high hopes in the victory of the kingdom see in small beginnings the mighty events that will follow, just like a father with his son.

Have the descendants of Abraham become as numerous as the stars of heaven or the sand of the sea? These are beyond calculation. Yet the promise was such. Was God exaggerating?

Is the bride of Solomon's Song really the only beauty, beside whom other girls are ugly? If not, why does the bridegroom say, "As a lily among thorns, so is my love among the daughters"?

I don't mind being accused of exaggeration when speaking passionately about the sufferings of the persecuted. When one tortured man cries, I hear more than one voice crying. All true believers suffer with the one who suffers. Jesus Himself suffers in them. Why do you hear only the cry of one insignificant man and not the cry of Jesus Who dwells within him?

How many suffer? How great is the suffering? Do you have good ears? When Abel was killed by his brother, his cry was so loud it reached from the ground to highest heaven (Gen. 4:10). Why then do you hold it against me that I hear one voice as the voice of a multitude?

I never exaggerate willingly, but neither am I a stickler for exact figures. Eichmann, the war criminal judged in Jerusalem for his participation in the Holocaust, gave as his defense: "Not six million but only one million Jews were killed by the Nazis." For me and my wife, who had family among the victims, the one million would never be only one million.

When all is said and done, anyone who now reads even Communist publications from the former USSR, Romania, and other Communist countries realizes that not only I, but also Solzhenitsyn, Bourdeaux and others are guilty of understatement.

Even now I have not told the whole story. Patrashcanu, the one who brought Communism to power in Romania, was later tortured by his own comrades in such a manner that I could never tell anyone, including my wife. No publisher would print such violent obscenities. It is strange that we can stand to see pictures of Jesus crucified, but we cannot stand to see the suffering of His saints.

Meanwhile, several newspapers and magazines in Europe have asked the World Council of Churches and the Lutheran World Federation to apologize to me. I absolve them of this obligation. But I would be gratified if they would take a stand against the atrocities committed today where Communists are still in power and would expel from their leadership those who have led people astray about non-existent religious liberty under the Reds unless they repent.

A Bleak Situation

After speaking in many services, I was invited to meals in the homes of believers.

In one very poor house my wife and I were served chicken, but from the expression on the faces of the children I realized they had never had such a thing. In Romania there is a proverb: "If a poor family eats chicken, either the chicken or the family is sick." We said we were not hungry and each took only a wing.

In other homes we were given good food, but we soon realized that it had been purchased on the black market for exorbitant prices and that the families would eat minimally after our departure. My own children, knowing for a long time that we would be in Romania, had hoarded food by standing in line for hours day after day, for weeks.

The Talmud says, "Every meal where the conversation is about something other than the word of God is idolatrous." I try to abide by this. Families have so little time to converse that mealtime should be used for spiritual as well as physical nourishment. But there were also jokes. A former member of the Communist Party said, "In times past, you had to be recommended by two members of the Party to be accepted. Now, only a certificate from a psychiatric asylum that you are mad is sufficient."

There was joy and happiness at meals in spite of the great poverty. But the situation was bleak, without any hope of improvement in the foreseeable future. I know the figures: in the first quarter of

1990, the productivity of workers and the gross
national product had decreased by 42% compared to
the year before. International trade had virtually
come to a standstill. There was no new capital infu-
sion into the economy. All socialist economic
planning went out the window. With no raw mate-
rial, many factories stand idle. Private enterprise is
now permitted, but where does one begin when
there is no capital? There are no goods for even the
smallest venture.

The transition from capitalism to socialism is
easy. You simply destroy what your predecessors
have accomplished. But the transition from
Communism to capitalism and the free market system has never yet taken place. Will it succeed? To
create or recreate a free market, capital is needed.
Historically, capitalism began in Europe because of
the huge amounts of gold discovered in America.

Where is Romania to obtain capital? The western capitalists have no confidence in the new
government because it represents no real change.
The leaders still feel free to slaughter innocents at
whim, just as their predecessors did. Between the
13th and 15th of June, 1990, a multitude of
corpses (no one knows how many) and countless
wounded, many mutilated for life, lay on the
streets of Bucharest. The killers were allegedly
miners, as reported in the western press, though the
people know they were men of the old *Securitate*
who wore miners' helmets as a disguise. These
"miners" had been called by President Iliescu
and were congratulated when they finished their
bloody work, because they had shown "proletarian
solidarity." Those were apocalyptic days. Hoards of

Communist police armed with iron sticks and axes roamed the streets killing people in the name of a government that called itself democratic. *Demon*ocratic would be more accurate. The image of such scenes persists long after the streets are cleared. People still hear the wild howling of the killers and the moaning of the wounded.

A sane economy, a free market system, cannot be built on such a foundation. Romania receives no substantial help from the West, unlike all the other Eastern European countries, which were also Communist. This was decided at a conference of twenty-four industrial nations in Brussels.

Capitalism and Communism

There were spiritual discussions at meals, along with songs and jokes, but no palpable hope for the immediate future of the country as far as living conditions are concerned. In view of all their bitter experiences with socialist economies, it is proper that Christians consider what their attitude should be in the conflict between capitalism and Communism. Wicked men cannot construct good social systems. Slavery, feudalism, capitalism, Communism— all are tainted with sin. However, the wise distinguish not only between good and bad, but also between good and better or between bad and worse.

Of all the social systems devised by men until now, Communism is surely the worst. One hundred and fifty years ago, Marx believed that capitalism would soon perish. Seventy years ago, Lenin believed in the near victory of the Communist revolution. In the United States, the great depression of the thirties was considered a sign that capitalism was on its deathbed. It was not. Capitalism has great vitality. Communism is sick.

Capitalism has proved to be the only system of production that by its very nature assures the development of new techniques that in turn raise the standard of living of the multitudes. Under capitalism, periods of crisis are followed by periods of recovery. Technical developments assure this. New discoveries result in new branches in the economy. Competition assures that products will become cheaper with time. The number of consumers grows. New enterprises are created and with them more jobs. The great number of unemployed in capitalist countries is due to the fact that job-seekers have not qualified themselves. For those who do and who are willing to work, joblessness is not generally a long-term problem under capitalism. In other words, there is no permanent crisis under capitalism.

Under socialism, by way of contrast, there can be no long periods of progress. No one is interested in investing capital because all the profit goes to the state. A political organism, the state, decides what factories should be built and how the goods should be distributed. It takes no advanced degree to observe that as a result the shops are almost always empty. Politicians decide on salaries. Romania provides a bitter example. During the election campaign in June 1990, the government announced a salary increase of 50% in many industries. Since all enterprises belong to the state, this was simple. After the elections, the same government that had used this ruse to win declared that no one in industry would have a fixed salary but rather it would be determined by productivity. However, since there is neither capital for productivity nor goods for even the most urgent repairs of machinery, industry is hobbled and workers are stymied.

Warning signals about the shape of the economy do not worry the planning commissions, who are the real bosses, because their members have no profit motive for what they do. They receive a modest salary whether or not the plan is fulfilled. Capitalists, on the other hand, react quickly to economic indicators because their capital is at stake. They can become millionaires or go broke. The profit incentive tends to prevent economic catastrophes. Under Communism, antiquated enterprises continue to function even though they bring no profit. The breakdown of Communism came in many countries without revolution. Romania was the exception. In Hungary, Czechoslovakia, Poland, East Germany, and Russia, Communism died a natural death because it simply doesn't work.

Capitalism has grave weaknesses, but it is the best system mankind has produced. Of necessity, Christians must prefer it to something far worse— Marxist economics. Nations that have tasted Communism now show their aversion to the system. In Romania, as in neighboring Eastern European countries, people have torn down the statues of Marx, Stalin, and Lenin with strong ropes and multiple manpower, so strong is their revulsion to the "gods" that have been imposed on them. Some are offered for good money to western collectors.

"Lord, when you awake, you will despise their image" (Ps. 73:20). Previously, pictures of Ceaushescu were seen everywhere. Now there is not one.

The Specter of Famine

Christians in Romania, like the rest of its inhabitants, have little time nowadays to think about heavy social or spiritual problems. The mere earning of daily bread consumes more than a normal man's power. And there is even worse danger for all former European Communist countries, and especially for Romania, which is excluded from aid from the USA and the European Community. Romania is also shunned by those who could invest capital because of the brutality and instability of its government, consisting almost exclusively of Communists who so far give few signs of having changed.

There is rampant inflation. The price of necessary goods has increased. Income is lower. Widespread unemployment is inevitable, since unproductive, inefficient factories kept alive by unreasonable state planners will have to be shut down. There is no legislation providing for the unemployed. All Christian charitable institutions have long since been abolished.

Meanwhile, the specter of famine towers over Romania. In winter there is not enough heat in the houses. Babies nurtured in a warm womb are born into cold hospital rooms and fall sick. In neighboring Hungary, also formerly Communist, Mother Theresa of Calcutta was allowed to open soup kitchens—but not in Romania. Leading specialists in economics, finance and industry have been dismissed because the public simply abhors Communists. Furthermore, other Communists in government sacrificed their comrades to the fury of the mob, with the result that the economy is ruled by ignoramuses.

The agricultural collectives are no longer productive. While no one really cares to work for them, who has the capital and machinery for individual farming? Former peasants would refuse land even if it were given back to them because they do not trust the Communists. Romanian peasants once owned land, and it was stolen from them by the Communists. So agriculture was destroyed. What warrant do they have that the Communists in power now, after allowing them to become productive again, would not take everything away from them a second time?

Whoever can manage to do so flees from Romania, not only German, Hungarian, and Jewish minorities, but also ethnic Romanians. But what country is ready to accept the millions hoping to emerge from the former Eastern bloc? Except for Christians, no one really knows in Romania (or Hungary, or Bulgaria, or Poland, or Russia) what to do. The believers know exactly what to do even under the worst circumstances: when one does not know what to do, it is imperative to do nothing, but with patience and trust to let God take over. He has known worse situations than these.

Not Everything Was Taken Away

When the Communists seized power, most of Romania was composed of small peasant holdings. The land was collectivized by the Communists who were inspired by Lenin's teaching: "We will introduce collectivization, not fearing coercion. Revolutions were never accomplished without coercion. The proletariat also has the right to use it to obtain its purpose in order to assure that its will is fulfilled."

Trotsky said, "Our peasantry is an ally of American millionaires. We cannot reach America, but we can suppress these with our cavalry, tanks and swords."

Bukharin, another leading Russian Communist theoretician, wrote, "Our party is the most militarily shaped organization."

In Romania, the Communists did indeed act militarily in taking away from the peasantry everything they owned: fields, sheep, cattle, implements, houses, furniture. Every small farmer became a slave of the state, working for a pittance on a field no longer his. Ceaushescu was one of the principal organizers of this collectivization. In Dobrogea province, he did it with the utmost simplicity. All the villagers were gathered together in a square and were asked to renounce their possessions of their own free will. "Who is for this?" No one raised his hand. So Ceaushescu personally shot ten people. Then the vote was taken a second time. All voted to renounce their possessions "voluntarily." There was military music. They were forced to dance. To add insult to injury, a film was made about their enthusiastic adherence to socialism.

With this, the agricultural sector of Romania was destroyed. In a country that formerly could feed all of western Europe, farmers were forced to stand in line for bread and were unable to obtain it. Now I met once more a farmer who had come to see me immediately after collectivization. He reported at that time, "They thought they took everything. But

I told my family, 'They left something very important—our hymnals.' We sat down and sang praises to the Lord."

I was reminded of those who "accepted joyfully the plundering of their goods, knowing that they have a better and enduring possession for themselves in heaven" (Heb. 10:34).

We embraced again. I, too, had known this joy several times in my life.

Hearing My Sermons Again

One of the most striking aspects of this visit to Romania was the encounters with brethren who said they had heard me preach thirty, forty, even fifty years before.

When someone tells me he heard a sermon of mine years ago, I always ask, "What did I say?" I believe that listening to a sermon should be an existential event, something that changes life for better or worse. In a sermon the preacher should not only speak *about* Christ but should *impersonate* Him. An actor does not speak *about* Hamlet or Romeo; he *is* the person while on stage. During those several hours in the theater his personal life is put aside completely. He speaks exactly as Romeo would speak if he encountered Juliet. Just so the minister. Not only by his words, but also by his gestures, by the expression on his face, by his appearance, his tone of voice, by the light of the Spirit shining through him, he must convey the impression, "I had an encounter with Jesus today. He speaks through me." Fifty years ago I heard just such an existential sermon, and today I could reproduce even the gestures of the bishop who delivered it.

When I became a preacher, I took seriously the words that we should "run so as to receive the prize" (1 Cor. 9:24). This is possible only by out-running all the others. So I read sermons by great preachers, listened to the best preachers of all denominations in Romania, and nurtured a desire to attain to their level and if possible surpass it.

I have not yet become the great preacher I intended to be (I still have hope—I am only eighty-two), but wanted to find out how much I had achieved. Therefore I asked those who said they had heard me half a century ago my usual question: "What did I say?" Some told me.

Telling a Legend

One sermon had begun with the legend of Gorun, a very beloved disciple of the Master. "There is good stuff in you," Jesus said to him. "I want you to pitch a tent for yourself on Mount Carmel and stay there for a time in meditation and prayer." And so he did.

Soon the rumor spread to all the villages round about that a young saint had made his habitation in the region.

One day Gorun went to the nearest village and begged, "Please give me a blanket. Rats have gnawed on my old one and they leave a bad smell. [I know this from my prison life.] Because of this I am unable to sleep."

The villagers gladly gave him what he asked. After a few days, he asked for another blanket because rats had gnawed on the second blanket, too. Soon he was back again with the same request, then again. Finally, someone said, "We'd

better give you a cat. That will solve the problem
for good."

Gorun returned happily to his abode. The rats
were no longer in control. But after two days he was
back. "Could you please give me some milk for the
cat?" The villagers were happy to comply. But the
need persisted. So they decided to give him a cow.

Again he came back. "I need something to feed
the cow." They decided to give him pasture land in
anticipation of future needs. Soon he came back. He
was not used to taking care of both land and animals,
so they gave him two workers to help him. Then he
needed bricks and materials to build houses for the
workers. Then the cow calved, and so on and on.

Years passed, and Jesus went to see his beloved
disciple. A fat man greeted him and asked, "What
business brings you to this place? What would you
like to buy?" The now well-to-do merchant no
longer recognized his Master.

Beginning with this legend, I had taught that we
should not put distance between us and Jesus, not
even so much as a stone's throw. Even at such a
small distance, disciples slept while Jesus agonized
in Gethsemane. Do business only if the Lord works
beside you with accompanying signs (Mark 16:20),
as He does in your Christian endeavors. If not, abandon the business.

Don't leave Jesus even for holy meditation or great
missionary deeds. To lie quietly on His breast like the
apostle John is preferable to the greatest enterprises in
His service. Whoever has once leaned on this breast
can no longer find full joy anywhere else.

Jesus said, "The first of all the commandments
is: 'Hear, O Israel' (Mark 12:29). Hear the beating

of my loving heart. Everything else follows from this."

Nothing should be preferred to loving gestures for the One Who leads us to eternal life. There is a depth in renunciation of everything else. The devil can tear one away from the life of a hermit on Carmel but not from the very breast of Christ. Blessed is the man who can do both his secular work and visible work for the church while lying spiritually on His breast. If he cannot do both, he should forego the work rather than the quiet adoration.

A brother of almost eighty repeated this sermon to me, heard fifty years before. He served me well. Curiously, I have no recollection of ever having read or heard the legend of Gorun. Yet I am told it was part of a sermon of mine. Perhaps I composed it myself. Legends are often good clothing for truth.

Count Your Seconds

Another person reminded me of a sermon thirty years old about Psalm 90:12. Again, I had started with a story (sermons without illustrations are not remembered).

A man was obliged to walk late at night to a village far away. The journey was monotonous, especially since it was dark and he could scarcely see the road. At a certain moment he stumbled on something in his path. Reaching down, he picked up a small bag full of pebbles. To distract himself from time to time he threw one in the river bordering the road on which he traveled. *Plitch . . . plitch. . . .* The sound of the splash was harmless amusement. When he reached his destination, only two pebbles remained. In the lighted house he glanced down and saw that they were diamonds. He had squandered a fortune.

Our days are made up of seconds. There are 32 million seconds in a year. A person who has lived thirty years is responsible for one billion. Every second comes to us from God as a gift to use in His service. If we do not, the second returns to God in sadness and reports that we have neglected His precious gift.

Then I told about a general in the former Royal Army with whom I had been in jail. He was very ill. When spoke to him about God, he showed no interest. But then his last hour came, and he asked for a priest. There were plenty of priests in that jail, but it took time to bring one from another cell. When he came, the general was no longer able to speak and make confession. The priest gave him Communion, but he could not swallow the wafer. He died without confession and Communion. He valued the treasure only when the last diamonds remained in the bag.

I spoke about how well Jesus used his seconds, even when crucified: pardon for his crucifiers, salvation to a robber, good words to his holy mother and to a beloved disciple, the assurance that all things needed for our salvation were fulfilled, a trusting prayer to God. Even in those dire circumstances, moments were not lost.

"Use your time well. Time is the most precious commodity. You can regain money lost but not time lost. Use your time in the Lord's service."

Physical Acts Communicate the Spirit

I visited Oradea, the city with the largest evangelical churches in Romania: a Baptist church led by

Dr. Gheorghitza and Pastor Negrutz, with 2,500 members attending, and a Pentecostal church with some 2,000. Space forbids my recounting all the things I preached in these churches, but I will mention one pronouncement that stunned the audience.

Ceaushescu is hated by the whole populace. I never heard one good word spoken about him. All speak evil of him, except Christians who have learned from the Arch-angel Michael not to dare to bring against even the devil a railing accusation (Jude 9). We often bring such accusations against men, even dead men. I was once warned in the night by a voice which said, "Don't speak evil against any dead persons. They hear us. If they are lost, they have pain enough. Don't add to it."

Now the congregation was anxious to hear my message. All eyes were fixed on me.

I spoke from John 20:22-23—"Jesus breathed on them, and said to them, 'Receive the Holy Spirit. If you forgive the sins of men, they are forgiven them.'"

"A physical act, a special manner of breathing," I continued, "can impart the Holy Spirit. At ordination, another physical act, the laying-on of hands, imparts the gifts of the Spirit. Bodies can be the tool of the Spirit, which can be communicated not only through words, but also through a really warm handshake, a loving look, a face expressing goodness and understanding, a brotherly kiss. A spiritual man should be such not only in words but in all his gestures."

I Defend Ceaushescu

Then I made my second point, to the stupefaction of my listeners: "Why did Jesus impart the Spirit to the apostles? He answers the question: that they may be able to forgive or retain sins.

"I regret not having been in Romania when Ceaushescu was judged. I would have volunteered to defend him."

It was obvious the audience could not believe their ears. I was reputed to be a fierce anti-Communist, having opposed Communism when even some of the best pastors had compromised their beliefs. Defend Ceaushescu? Out of the question! Not only had he and his wife been killed, to everyone's satisfaction, but all his children, brothers, and in-laws were in jail. To bear the name Ceaushescu was crime enough.

I went on to explain: "I was in jail with a former major in the police during Fascist times. His sentence was twenty years. He claimed to be a Christian, blessed himself the whole time with the sign of the cross, and prayed to God, the Virgin, and a number of other saints.

"This man was sentenced for having arrested during the war (in the early forties Romania was at war with the Soviet Union) a lad of fourteen who had distributed Communist leaflets, then strictly forbidden. This lad was a member of an atheist organization, the Communist Youth.

"What an occasion this was for a Christian! The major should have seated the young lad and taken the opportunity to show him lovingly how wrong he was. He should have pointed him to a better way, the way of Christ.

"Instead, he beat the boy savagely. With every lash he inflicted, he strengthened in him his atheist convictions and confirmed his hatred for God.

"The name of that young boy was Nicolae Ceaushescu. Some of the foremost criminals of history—Hitler, Stalin, Lenin, Marx—also had early encounters with Christians who had not used the occasion well.

"At a certain moment, the guards threw into my cell a Catholic priest who had been beaten badly and was bleeding. We washed him as best we could and gave him water to drink.

"When he came to himself I asked him, 'Can you pray, like Jesus. "Father, forgive them, for they know not what they do"?'

"He replied, 'Jesus could, I cannot. My prayer would rather be, "Father, forgive me and them, because if I had been a better priest, they might not have become torturers."'

"'I would have told the court which judged the Ceaushescu all this,' I went on, 'and would have concluded: "Judge for yourselves if you have no part in their crimes."' Then I challenged the audience: 'You judge yourselves and ask if you have done your utmost to share with the Communists the teaching of Jesus and to turn them from their wicked ways.'

"In 1918, the Russian Communists killed Czar Nicholas II, his wife, his four daughters, the twelve-year-old crown prince, and their servants. After the murder they found in the house a handwritten poem from the pen of Princess Olga, aged fifteen:

> On the threshold of the grave,
> Put on the lips of Your servants
> Superhuman power to pray humbly
> For our enemies.

"This too I would have quoted to the judges. May we all learn the beautiful art of forgiveness."

There were tears in the eyes of many in the congregation.

"Gorbachev, Remember Ceaushescu's Lot!"

Obviously I was not able to appear in court to defend Ceaushescu. He and his wife Elena had both been sentenced to death. She was executed. He was badly tortured to get him to reveal where he had deposited—abroad—the millions he had allegedly stolen from the country. He is said to have died of a heart attack during the torture. His corpse was shot and displayed on public TV.

Ceaushescu's death frightened other Communist dictators and their stooges. The president of the court that had sentenced him committed suicide one week later. In East Germany, seven generals of the *Stasi*, their Secret Police, also committed suicide. These are known. No one knows how many of their subalterns did the same thing. There were many suicides among the officers of the Soviet KGB as well.

On the 15th of July, the Russian magazine *Gudok* reported on a demonstration in Moscow with an estimated attendance of 400,000.

There were posters with messages that were unthinkable a year ago: "Down with the Communist Party!" "Down with the KGB!" "Communism is the scourge of the twentieth century." "The Communist Party consists of henchmen and deceivers." And so on.

But the most striking slogan was: "Gorbachev, remember Ceaushescu's lot!" There was another praising Fanny Kaplan, a girl who in 1921 had wounded Lenin in an attempt on his life.

A member of the Supreme Soviet, Murashov, delivered a speech in which he said: "We don't want a restructuring *(perestroika)* of Communism. No reforms, no changes. Communism should perish. The Romanians did well with Ceaushescu."

A general of the KGB, Oleg Kalughin, joined the ranks of the opponents of Gorbachev. He declares he has become a democrat, but the opponents don't believe him. They ask him to enumerate the crimes committed in his career that allowed him to rise to the rank of general. In the debates in the press about him, it is suggested that he and others have changed sides only because of the fate of Ceaushescu. What happened to him also frightened the Communist dictators of Albania, Mongolia, Korea, and Ethiopia, who began to take steps to come to terms with their own people. Romanian blood shed for the cause of liberty by martyrs of the revolution has had wide-ranging effects.

Do We Need Two Religions?

In Oradea, I had one of my most memorable encounters. I met my former fellow-inmates Pastor Visky, Pastor Szöke, and others from the so-called Bethanists, a revival movement within the Hungarian-speaking Reformed Church. Several members of this group, theological students as well as pastors, along with pastors of the Hungarian Unitarian Church, were in one huge cell together with Catholic and Orthodox priests, some sixty or seventy in all. Each confession gathered separately, with no common fellowship in Christ. Instead, there were heated debates, not so much about which religion was right but about what was wrong with another's religion.

The story is told of a lone survivor of a shipwreck who made it to a desert island where he lived like Robinson Crusoe. Two years later, when he was discovered, his rescuers were surprised to find that he had built two prayer houses. "Why would you, alone on an island, build even one prayer house, let alone two?" they asked.

"Every man needs two religions," he explained. "One that he is for and one that he is against."

What was the essential question we debated in our overcrowded cell?

The essence of religion cannot be the subject of debate. If it is, the debaters reveal their ignorance. Religion is life, adoration, silence. Though words may indeed be spoken, it is not in the English sense of the expression "word."

The Hebrew word for "word," *davar*, also means "the real thing." In Hebrew, John's Gospel reads: "In the beginning was *Davar*, 'the real thing,' and 'the real thing' was with God, and 'the real thing' was God." The verb "to speak" in Hebrew is *ledaber*, from the root *davar* in its sense of giving a real thing. Even in Greek the word *logos* has both meanings.

Unhappily, at that time I too got caught up in the debates, but I remember telling the following Jewish joke. A young couple went to a rabbi to obtain a divorce. Among Christians, people go to the pastor or priest only for weddings, but in Judaism a rabbi is needed for divorces as well. The astonished rabbi responded, "I married you only a year ago, and you seemed so much in love with each other. Why do you want a divorce now?"

The woman replied, "Let's not waste any time. Reconciliation is useless. Just go through the formality. That's all we want. At this point talk is superfluous."

The rabbi insisted: "At least satisfy my curiosity. What happened? What is the reason for divorce?"

The man said, "We had a child, a boy."

"That's no reason for divorce."

"Yes it is, because we cannot agree on a name for him."

"What name did you choose?"

"I chose 'Nahum,'" he replied.

"Very good—the name of a prophet. But why did you choose this name?"

"Because it was the name of my father."

"Even better. You wish to honor your parent."

The rabbi then turned to the woman. "What name do you wish to give your son?"

She replied, "Nahum."

Surprised, the rabbi asked, "Why did you choose this name?"

"My father's name was also Nahum."

The rabbi couldn't help asking, with wonder, "If you both want the same name for the same reason, why do you quarrel?"

The man replied, "My wife is shrewd. I wish to call him Nahum for my father and she for hers. But her father was a horse thief and mine was a sage."

This is the impression I get of religious squabbles among Christians. All Christians want to glorify God's name, work for the coming of His kingdom, spread the gospel and the message of His love, and more. Then let us love one another!

The rabbi counseled the couple, "Call him Nahum after the prophet. Then live together happily for some twenty years. By that time, if your son becomes either a rabbi or a thief, you will know which parent's name he bears. Why start the quarrel now?"

In the divided cell, it took a long time for us to persuade even the priests of the two Catholic Churches, Roman and Byzantine Rite, to say an "Our Father" together.

A Christlike Pastor

During all this mental, physical and spiritual anguish, Pastor Visky was a unique example to us. Many considered him the most Christlike among us. During the time when we had one small slice of bread a day with some soup of potato peels or rotten carrots, he would give half of his bread to a sick, weak or older prisoner. Once I remember he shared a sweater with a fellow prisoner. His words were always pleasant, and a smile did not disappear from his lips.

As for the rest of us, we were happy if we chanced to observe in him some little sign of irritation or a harsh word, because we knew then that we still had a chance with God. We reasoned that if a Christian had to be as advanced in holiness as Pastor Visky to be acceptable to God, our chances were nil. He retained this composure though he suffered more than us. Somehow he had received news that his wife and seven small children had been deported to a barren part of the country where not only food but also water were lacking.

In Gethsemane, where Peter was ready to defend Jesus with a sword, he said to the disciples, "Permit even this." The worst must be accepted with composure and even with joy. Now I had the joy of meeting Visky and his family. Our mission had supported such families through secret channels in Romania and several other Communist countries. He expressed deep gratitude to all donors who helped him survive.

Which Is the True Biography?

First there was just small talk, but then he gave me the outline of a book on his prison experiences that he was writing. I could not believe my ears. All the beautiful attitudes and laudatory deeds I had said about him as illustrations in my sermons, he attributed to me. Bemused, I asked him, "Was it you or I? Which of us is telling the truth?" Then I knew the answer. It was simply what minds with great love, true attachment, and holy fantasy see in their beloved.

Never believe biographies. If they are written by adversaries, they tell not what the man truly was but what enmity, rancor, or jealousy saw in him. If they are written by admirers, they will reveal the noble heart of the biographer, who ornaments the subject of his book with his own virtues. As for "objective" biographies that tell the story with pedantic exactitude and thrifty dosages of praise or criticism, don't waste your time reading them. They are boring, worth nothing.

Truth is truth only when told by the passionate. The original of the New Testament had no punctuation marks. It is up to us to decide how to punctuate

John. 14:6, where Jesus says, "I am the way the truth and the life." I would suggest the following: "I am the way: the truth and the life." Those who think like Him never offer prosaic truth by itself, but animate it with the beautiful passions of lives worth living.

Visky's children, who grew up in utter misery, are all believers now, some engineers, some pastors, every one in some useful work for the kingdom. Men like Visky brought love, peace and light to shepherds at loggerheads with one another, even in a prison cell where all suffered for the same Savior. But this common suffering was worthwhile. Christians learned in time to understand and admire each other.

Now in 1990, Romanian Christians have formed for the first time in history an evangelical alliance, which includes Baptists, Lutherans, Pentecostals, Brethren, and the Army of the Lord. The latter, with an estimated membership of 800,000, is the cream of the Orthodox Church.

The Roman Catholic Church is not in the alliance, but relations with it are correct and friendly. The enmity of past times no longer exists. One side does not call the other "idolaters" and the other does not respond with "heretics." The Catholic archbishop Robu is the only head of a denomination who, in his sermons, took a public stand against the murder of innocents instigated by the new president Iliescu.

The Most Persecuted

As for the Byzantine Rite Catholic Church (1.5 million members), also known as Uniates, we all admire the heroism in faith of their members. Almost all its bishops and many priests died in jail after severe torture. Their jail sentences totaled 600 years. All their church buildings, schools, and charitable institutions were stolen from them by the Communists and given to the Orthodox Church, whose hierarchy was foremost in collaborating with the Reds.

The crime against the Uniate Church has not been repaired even now. The government has assured them that in principle they are completely free. But how can 1.5 million people enjoy religious freedom when deprived of all their buildings? Stolen property has not yet been returned.

The Uniate church has a history of two hundred years of great suffering. The church began in the eighteenth century in the Romanian province of Transylvania, at that time under the domination of the Austro-Hungarian monarchy of the Hapsburgs. It was a split from the Orthodox church, to which most Romanians belong. The Uniates retained all the Orthodox rituals but accepted all the dogmas of the Catholic church. Composed only of Romanians, it suffered in Transylvania all the vexations to which the nation was subjected under the years of Hungarian rule. The church enjoyed freedom for only thirty years, from 1918 when Transylvania united with Romania until 1956 when the Communists abolished it.

The second most persecuted group is the Army of the Lord whose very existence had not been recognized, either by the state or by the Orthodox church subservient to the state until late in 1990.

My First Encounter with Jesus

How can I tell all that I experienced in Romania? One day as a boy, with deep emotion I entered an

Orthodox church in Bucharest. It was the first Christian church I had ever seen on the outside. Brought up by non-practicing Jewish parents, I never heard in my childhood either a bad or a good word about Jesus. He was simply unknown to me.

One day as I returned home from school with another boy, he stopped in front of this church and said, "Wait for me a minute. My father asked me to tell the priest something." I said, "No, I'll go in with you." This is how I crossed the threshold of a church for the first time.

I was deeply impressed. Now, re-entering the same church after some seventy years, I relived vividly my initial experience.

As a child I saw a picture of a man crucified. I had no idea who this man was, but thought he must have been very bad or this would not have been done to him. As a child I was much spanked and probably deserved it. But this man, bleeding all over, attached with nails to a cross—why?

I also saw at that time a picture of a beautiful young lady, who looked at me with great love. I was not accustomed to such an expression. I was despised for being a Jewish boy, and was also very poorly dressed, thin, frail, small. This lady loved me. I loved her, too, from that moment.

I wonder why some Christians never think of Mary with love. The Bible says "all generations will call her blessed." Why don't we?

Reason tells me that I did not actually see the Cucified One or that lady, but only a representation. At that time I had the impression that I was seeing real persons. It was one of the several existential events in my life.

The other boy spoke with the priest, who then came to me and caressed me on the head. It meant much to me, since my parents were not demonstrative. He had a fine touch, the kind I felt at my ordination. Bishop Argay really loved me. Only ordinations performed by those with divine love impart gifts of the Holy Spirit.

As the priest caressed me, he asked, "Little fellow, what can I do for you?"

I was embarrassed, thinking perhaps I was not permitted to be in that strange place. I replied, "Nothing."

He said, "That can't be. I belong to Jesus, who taught us not to allow anyone to pass near us without doing him some good. It is summertime and it is hot outside. I will bring you a cup of cold water."

Jesus—what a strange being! To that point no one I had met knew anything of His teachings. I was given no toys, no chocolate. (When other children ate chocolate, I licked the paper in which it was wrapped.) Jesus changed the water I received into wine. I was stunned.

Being young, I soon forgot this incident. But when I became a Christian, it came back to my memory. The name of that priest was Cavane.

Many years later when I was an evangelical pastor, the Fascists came to power. A new priest in that church, Chiricuta, was the only Orthodox priest who allowed me, a Protestant and, even worse, a Jew, to preach regularly at evensong in his church. He was unconcerned that other priests bullied him for this. I became a contributor to his Orthodox magazine.

During the war, when my wife and I and several

other Hebrew Christians were court-marshaled, he dared to offer himself as a defense witness. He defended a Jew when Hitler ruled Europe! His defense and that of a German Baptist pastor resulted in ours being the only case in which Jews were acquitted under Hitler. Normally, we would have been condemned, whether guilty or not guilty.

Now, back in Romania after an absence of twenty-five years, I was able to pray in that same church, remembering how much good God had done to me there. God surely has a reward for the one who offered a cup of cold water and unconditional love in His name.

Anti-Semitism

Only some 15,000 Jews have remained in Romania, which at one time had a Jewish population of 600,000. Many of those—among them my wife Sabina's family—perished in the Holocaust. Quite a few have emigrated to Israel and other countries. But even this small remnant wants to leave the country now. The stirrings of anti-Semitism, which were stifled under Ceaushescu, are evident again.

Why didn't this dictator persecute the Jews? Because no one persecutes a cow that gives him milk. The Jews were a great source of income for the government. They were sold to the state of Israel, sometimes at very high prices, depending on their qualifications. The sale of Jews to Israel and ethnic Germans to West Germany enriched the treasury and—it is said—Ceaushescu personally. Anti-Semitic publications were forbidden.

Now the situation has changed in Eastern Europe. There is *glasnost* and relative freedom of speech. So anti-Semites are free to reveal the hatred they have in their hearts for Jews.

The Romanian president Iliescu is a former school colleague and personal friend of Gorbachev, who has shown how he feels about Jews by naming to his presidential council Valentin Rasputin (the name means "profligate" in Russian and gained notoriety in the person of an immoral monk who was an intimate adviser to the Russian imperial family). In an interview given to the *New York Times Magazine*, Rasputin said, "Our Jews must feel responsibility for the sins of the revolution and for its consequences . . . responsibility for the terror that existed during the revolution and especially after it. . . . Their guilt is great, for they killed God and also Russians."

It is moving to read how painful it is for this high-ranking leader of a God-hating regime to think of God being killed when He came to earth. Certain Jews of old did play a role in the death of Jesus. It was because He Himself was a Jew and lived in Israel. Curiously, I never heard accusations against the Greek people for having killed Socrates or the Italian nation for having persecuted Galileo.

The interview with Rasputin was published in January 1990. In March he was named to Gorbachev's presidential council. This was his reward. Some knew what conclusion to draw from this interview. In the Moscow magazine *Nedelia* (16/1990), one person proposed a simple solution to the Jewish problem. If everyone who understands the Jewish danger would free the country of one single Jew, tomorrow there would be no more Jews. Certainly a program to which Ayatollah Khomeini and the leaders of the Lebanese terrorist organization Hezbollah would subscribe.

"Nothing distorts human nature so much as maniacal ideas. If a man is possessed by the idea that all evil in the world comes from the Jews, Masons, Bolsheviks, heretics, capitalists, etc., even the best man becomes a wild beast." So wrote Berdiaev.

One can choose among many accusations against the Jews: "Christianity is a Jewish ideology into which nations have been tricked to create a Judeo-Christian civilization, so that in the end the whole world will become an enlarged Israel."

"Communists were right in fighting capitalism, but they did not say who is guilty of it: the Jews."

"Columbus was a Jew who discovered America with the purpose of making it a center of Zionism from which the Jews would dominate the world through the dollar."

"International Communism was also created by the Jew Marx for the purpose of destroying love for one's nation and fatherland." And so on.

This anti-Jewish propaganda could not be spread in the USSR without the connivance of Gorbachev's government.

From the Soviet Union, anti-Semitism spreads to other countries just freed from the shackles of Communism. All are passing through a grave economic crisis. In Romania, the new government has declared it will no longer subsidize the prices of bread, milk, meat, etc., which means prices may soon rise by 50%. In times of crisis people need to blame someone, and the Jews provide a convenient scapegoat. For two thousand years of history this has been the case.

Some of the Romanian Communist leaders were Jewish: Ana Pauker, Kishinevski, Rautu, along with some of the leaders of the Secret Police. That the majority were Romanians or Hungarians doesn't matter; the Jews are guilty.

While it is true that Roman, the first prime minister after the revolution, was a Jew, it must be remembered that Marx himself was also a Jew and a Jew-hater.

Romanian anti-Semites who are also anti-Hungarians are grouped under the name *Vatra Romaneasca* "The Romanian Home."

Romanian Jews, as well as those in other Eastern European countries, are concerned. But where should they go? The USA does not receive them. In Israel, Arabs kill Jews and there is always imminent danger of war. In Romania there are Jewish Christian efforts to acquaint Jews with their King, Jesus. Many are from the province of Bessarabia, theater of the Second World War. They remember that when the Nazi army entered, posters were seen everywhere: "Calamities come from the dirty Jews"; "Jews have provoked this war"; "Jews are behind Communism"; "Death to the Jews." And the Jew-haters did not only threaten. Rare are the Jewish families from that province who had no relatives executed by firing squads or deported to concentration camps. Almost the whole of my wife's family (both parents, three sisters, and a brother aged six) perished in such a camp. Since the situation in Romania cannot be assessed apart from the rest of Eastern Europe and especially the Soviet Union, a few words are in order about the latter.

Gorbachev a Blessing

Gorbachev has been a blessing for the western world. Just imagine the Gulf crisis with the USSR and the West opposed to each other, as in the cold war!

When, during the thirties, Stalin killed all the high command of his own army, suspecting them of intrigue against him, Italy's Fascist dictator Mussolini wrote, "Stalin is a disguised Fascist." Gorbachev was hardly an agent of the American CIA, but he has done its work well. He undermined the power of the Soviet Union and with it the power of Communism in the whole of Eastern Europe. The western Communist Parties have also been shattered.

I remember how, when I arrived in the USA, the general secretary of the World Council of Churches begged me not to publish the atrocities of Communism. But Gorbachev caused them to be publicized. Today you can read in the Soviet newspapers about the millions of innocents killed and about the whole populace being robbed, exploited, and oppressed by the Communists.

But while he himself exposes the cataclysm Communism brought to Russia, Communist Leaders, nicknamed the *nomenklatura*, still cling to power. They acknowledge they have nothing to give to the people, yet they continue to wield power and, begging money from the capitalists, they lead Russia to tragedy, a bloodbath that might surpass everything history has known till now.

Perhaps they are guided by the instinct of self-preservation. Or perhaps they have simply abandoned planning and thinking about a more distant future.

Though Gorbachev played a leading role in the preparation of the drama, he himself would be better suited to play the actor in a farce. He presided over the dismantling of his Party and of the Soviet Union itself, yet ended the congresses by singing the "Internationale," the venerable hymn of Communism. He and his cohorts chant about fighting to the end the deadly battle that will give the whole world the "ideal" society that is now in its death throes in its homeland, Russia. Their slogan is still "Proletarians of the world, unite!" Then they decide at their congresses that the Ukrainian, Russian, Byelorussian, Baltic, and Uzbek Communists should go their separate ways. These decisions only help to enhance extreme nationalism. The result will be a new brand of Fascism, or, more likely, several brands of Fascism, because each of the Soviet republics will have its own to foster against others. Gorbachev and his ilk have played a major role in emasculating Soviet and Eastern European Communism. Without intending to do so, they have rendered the free world a great service, putting off for a time the threat of war between East and West.

Yeltsin, also a former Communist leader, though in personal conflict with Gorbachev, walks the same way.

Should Christians Be in Politics?

Before going further, I feel I must reply to a frequently heard and pertinent question. Should a Christian, and especially a pastor, depart from the Bible and speak out on political matters? This question is very acute for Romanian Christians as well. Some claim we should speak out on political issues, while others say we shouldn't. Somehow they don't realize that by speaking out fervently about not making politics, they are playing the political game. Why don't they use their energy to explain the atonement of Christ or the doctrine of the Trinity?

The word "politics" comes from the Greek *polis*, meaning city. "Alms" is doing good to a few men, "philanthropy" is doing good to many, and "politics" is the art of doing good to a nation and even beyond.

Some 70% of the Bible is concerned with politics: the constitution of a nation, its liberation from slavery, the multitude of its wars against other nations, laws regarding social relations, agriculture, hygiene, matrimony, inheritance, the establishment of monarchies and the rivalries among them, along with the misdeeds of rulers, much as the media would expose them today.

"Give to Caesar what is Caesar's" is political advice, as is incitement to rebellion. "Be submissive to authorities" is also political advice, along with descriptions by Daniel and the Revelation of world rulers as ferocious beasts.

We have to evaluate political events to find our way through them. Many discussions among Romanian Christians were not only about the ascent of the soul from the earthly to the angelic, which is holiness, but also about political events in the country and under Communism in particular.

Preaching Under Escort

Another place with powerful memories for me is the Baptist church in Giuleshti, a suburb of Bucharest. I had been invited to preach there the first

Sunday after Romania entered the Second World
War, in 1941. At that time the Nazis dominated our
country, and when their army attacked Russia, it was
in alliance with our troops. The slogan was,
"Destroy Communism created by the dirty Jews.
Beat the Jews!"

I went to church with a group of other Hebrew
Christians. The brethren had invited many unbe-
lievers, telling them who would be the preacher. The
Baptists were already hated by the Orthodox. Now
something even worse was about to take place: a
Jew would preach in the pulpit of the despised
Baptist sect. Anti-Semites could not stomach the sit-
uation. They denounced this intolerable crime to the
police, and we six Hebrew Christians were arrested.
A Romanian Christian lady, Sister Mindrutz,
knocked at the gate of the prison where my wife and
I and the four other Jews were detained and said,
"My brethren from the chosen people suffer here for
Christ. I wish to suffer with them." Her demand was
graciously accepted. She was put in the same cell
with us. Now we were seven: three Jews, three
Jewesses, and the Romanian.

The cell was small, with only one single bed. The
police officer said, "You priest (meaning me), will
sleep in the bed and all the others on the floor."

Meanwhile, the Orthodox priest of Giuleshti
went to the police to make sure that we would not be
freed. He also spoke with me to convince me that
there was no place for Jews in Christianity. At that
time, the patriarchy had forbidden the baptism of
Jews.

Following the Giuleshti arrest we were taken to
the prison of the Military Tribunal for interrogation.

While we were being questioned, the air raid alarm sounded. Bucharest was being attacked by Soviet planes. Soldiers with bayonets on their rifles escorted us to the basement, along with our investigators, the staff of the Tribunal, our prosecutors and future judges. We prisoners were kept in a corner under strict surveillance. The conversation of the others was about trifles. One young lady complained about a new garment she had not yet worn—and now the bombing!

Then the first bombs were heard falling. The explosions shook the earth. Weeping and panic broke out. Seizing the opportunity, I said with authority, "You have a pastor among you. I will give you a word of comfort from Scripture, and then we will pray. Please kneel."

Everyone knelt, including guards, prosecutors, and judges. I was then able to speak to them from the word of God.

When the bombing was over, we were taken back to our cells, escorted again by soldiers with bayonets they would not hesitate to use if we attempted to escape. Those who had knelt at my command half an hour before were again my prosecutors and judges.

I relived all these events on seeing the Malmezon prison. What I have just recounted took place in Fascist times. Later, under the Communists, I was again a guest in this same prison.

A Spiritual Experience

In one of its solitary cells, I had had a spiritual experience to which I alluded in several sermons delivered in Romania upon my recent return. I say "alluded" because a deep spiritual experience cannot be adequately expressed in any language. One enters into contact with a reality that is neither namable nor explainable. Therefore, the Bible is God's revelation in both senses of the word: it reveals something so that we may perceive it, but it also reveils it.

Explaining what you experience often does little good. Beethoven had experiences and put them in music. A sculptor in Buenos Aires carved for a cemetery nine statues symbolizing the nine symphonies. After I had visited the site, someone asked me to explain what the statues were. Sentiments had become music, which then became sculpture, which needed words for interpretation. How much of a relationship would these words have had with Beethoven's experiences?

The Bible says, "Taste and see that the Lord is good" (Ps. 34:8). No speech, no music, could explain to you the difference between the taste of a watermelon and a peach. Only tasting works.

We can hint at spiritual experiences but only with the aim of encouraging others to have their own. Put through the filter of words, such experiences are diminished in value. Everyone has to make an individual effort to obtain the capacity to see reality beyond appearance.

A Zen master was asked by a disciple, "What is Buddha?" He replied, "This flax weighs three pounds"—another way of saying, "What Buddha is cannot be expressed in words. Let us spend our time better by talking about practical things."

If Buddha cannot be expressed in words, even less can Jesus.

Timelessness

I have spent years in solitary confinement in three different prisons. While there, I lost track of time. Our solitary cells had only a window facing the corridor, none on the outside. We never knew if it was bitter winter or beautiful spring. We could not tell night from day. The same electric bulb burned constantly. Probably for the purpose of confusing us, the prisons had no fixed program of hours when they would awaken prisoners, give them food, or allow them to go to the toilet. We were time-disoriented.

We lived in timelessness as astronauts live in weightlessness. If prolonged for years, timelessness produces a state of mind apart, not comprehensible intellectually. Our senses had nothing to sense. Perfect silence reigned. We almost never heard a voice or a whisper, and the guards wore felt-soled shoes. There was nothing to see. We were surrounded by the same gray walls. We forgot that colors exist. The stench was overpowering and unrelenting, to the point of paralyzing the olfactory nerve. To this day I cannot smell the perfume of flowers. As for taste, the food was always bland and bad and always the same.

Our minds were not oriented to the senses or regulated by logic.

As I tried to relive those days on my return to Romania as a free man, it was difficult to interpret those experiences for contemporary ears as I spoke in churches. However, being Jewish helps when it comes to timelessness.

Biblical Hebrew does not have our tenses: I eat, I ate, I have eaten, I had eaten, I will eat, I will have eaten, and so on. God's people are not intended to cut time in pieces: past, present and future. This dividing of time is not natural. The past is not only past; it lives very much in the present, often carrying with it joy or sadness. It will also live in the future. The basis of today and tomorrow is what has been accumulated in the past. Some of the past was also determined by the previous perspective of the future. We are part of one undivided ocean in which waves flow back and forth but remain part of the same ocean. And so as I gazed at the prison walls that had contained me and thought of what went on below, I tried to relive old experiences.

Crucified for You Today

How easy it is for one who can divide time to accept salvation. I can be forgiven of all my sins and obtain heaven by believing that Jesus died for me a long time ago. He chose to suffer for me without asking me. He suffered on the cross for a few hours and then died. On the third day He was resurrected, then returned to heaven, where He has lived now for two thousand years. It would give Him great joy if I was converted. Then why shouldn't I become a Christian? It would give us mutual joy. Many people come forward during evangelistic appeals with a smile on their face. In great crusades, few tears are shed.

With us, dwelling in timelessness, it was otherwise. Everything was experienced only in the present. Golgotha did not belong to the past but was a present event. It was as if Jesus was standing before me, saying, "You have sinned. For you I will be whipped and crucified. Before your very eyes you will see and hear nails being driven into my flesh. You will see my holy mother weeping at the foot of the cross. Do you accept this my actual sacrifice for you, or do you prefer to bear the punishment of your sins yourself?"

The crucifixion was no longer an old story read in a book. I had to decide then and there who should die: Barabbas or Jesus. Peter, John, and Mary Magdalene did not have to accept a past sacrifice of Christ, but one in the present or near future. No guilty person with a sense of decency would allow himself to be the eyewitness of the actual cruel death of someone else for what he had done. Neither could we in solitary confinement.

Now I relived what I understood then. It was never intended that salvation should be the result of His dying for me, period. There is no period after His death, not even a comma. We are meant to be "crucified and buried together with him" (Rom. 6:6), which is something entirely different.

Luther called the book of James "an epistle of straw" because it teaches that faith alone without deeds is not sufficient. He was wrong. "We are saved by faith"—no period after this assertion. We have to add many sacrifices to this faith (2 Peter 1:5-8). It is a sacrifice to remain always pure, loving, forgiving, active in God's service. We have to fill up what is lacking in the cross of Christ.

The priest Cheruvian did so. Forced after unspeakable torture to give a Satanist Communion, pronouncing the holy words "This is My body" and "This is My blood" over human excrement and urine, he later told me, "I have suffered more than Christ." As far as physical torture was concerned, perhaps this is true.

In timelessness, we lived simultaneously the passion of Christ, His resurrection, His ascension, and His final triumph.

In that solitary cell, we were also concerned not only with the earthly life of men but with their eternal life as well. Death is not an end. In timelessness, we also experienced the afterlife.

Where is Ceaushescu Today?

With these thoughts in mind, I preached again in Romanian churches. I asked my listeners, "Where are the Ceausescus today? He was not able to finish his last speech. The audience booed him and he fled. But now he speaks again. Don't you hear him?

"In Jesus' parable, the rich man in hell begged Abraham to send someone to his brothers to tell them not to lead lives that would bring them to the same place of torment. He was refused; he had asked the wrong man. Abraham had been very harsh with Hagar, mother of his own child. He expelled her from his house with only a loaf of bread and a skin full of water. Why should he show pity to those in hell?

"But perhaps Ceaushescu petitions Jesus, with whom he has a better chance. The rich man was not totally wicked. At least he had love for his lost brothers. Perhaps Ceaushescu too loves some of his old Communist comrades. Perhaps he asks each of us now, 'Go to other Communists and tell them that I suffer the fire and brimstone of condemnation. Warn them to seek another Way.'

"Whoever has experienced timelessness or, in better words, reality beyond the temporal, hears not only the songs of cherubim and seraphim calling him, but also the howling of those in despair in hell. And there is something even more unbearable to listen to: the deep silence of those kept in darkness (1 Sam. 2:9).

"The silence of some pleads from hell, 'Tell the good news to the worst of men. Think about their terrible destiny. Jesus is interested in them. He proved it by descending into hell.'"

There were unusual strains in my Romanian sermons. I thank God they were well received. For these moments of triumph in my homeland, I had passed through much suffering and sickness and perils of all kinds. It was all by God's grace.

A Sign from God

In the case of Chinese women over seventy, mortality diminishes by 35% before the harvest feast. In the week following, it returns to normal. This has been established in the studies of the death dates of Chinese-Americans in California. The expectation of a feast, the sentiment of duty to help prepare for it, can influence mortality. With Orthodox Jews, mortality diminishes before the Passover feast and returns to normal during the week following.

Epidemiological research reports only on physical, chemical, and psychological factors that influence mortality. Religion has its influence too. My wife and I believed that God would prove that we were justified in our fight, in which we had encountered much opposition and contradiction. He would give us a sure sign. We willed not to die before revisiting the old places, bearing triumphantly the banner of Christ. More were on our side than the enemy's. I revisited Romania and its churches at the age of eighty-two. I will not disclose my wife's age, but she too knew the triumph when well advanced in years.

Romania Not Yet Whole

What one sees on the map is not the whole of Romania. The vicissitudes of history have caused much of the nation to live outside its boundaries.

In 1939, when Hitler and Stalin divided up Eastern Europe, Russia obtained the Romanian provinces of Bessarabia and Bucovina. The Red Army occupied them at the end of the Second World War. The Soviets renamed Bessarabia "Moldavia" and invented a language that the Bessarabian Romanians were obliged to use. To do so, they mixed Romanian with a number of Russian words and then required that the result be written in the Cyrillic alphabet of Russian instead of the Latin alphabet used in the West. Romanians are the only Latins of Eastern Europe, but they were forbidden to use their own alphabet.

Bulgaria also stole from Romania—the province of Cadrilater. To the east of Bessarabia is Transnistria, another territory thickly populated by Romanians. The province of Banat, in Yugoslavia, is ethnically Romanian, as is the language spoken there. We hope this whole territory will be reunited with the motherland once and for all under our beloved King Michael I. It should certainly be the concern of the Romanian churches.

It is a special sorrow to me that the Bible, even the New Testament, has not yet been translated into the Macedo-Romanian language spoken by a compact Romanian minority in Greece, Bulgaria, Yugoslavia, and Albania. Lydia, the first Christian in

Europe, was a Macedonian (Acts 16:12-14). Her language must have been Macedo-Romanian, which is nothing but a dialect of Romanian, but the difference is still so great that an uncultured Macedo-Romanian would not understand a plain Romanian Bible. It would be like Languedocian and French, Frizian and Dutch, Swiss-German and German, though the Swiss-German, being cultured, would know classical German. European Christians owe it to the memory of Lydia, the first European Christian, to care about the translation of the Bible into Macedo-Romaman.

Romanian Martyrs

Romanian Christians also miss much through the lack of communication with Bessarabia. This eastern province, stolen by the USSR, is known for its many wonderful Christians.

The renowned martyr, Vania Moiseev, was from that area. In spite of his Russian name, he was Romanian and did not even know the Russian language. The Soviets have Russified Romanian names. Moisiu was renamed Moiseev. He had been a soldier in the Red Army. He had the same faith that we have, with one difference: his faith was contagious. True faith is like the flu. If you have the flu, it is catching. So is faith. In his regiment, soldiers and officers were converted.

His superiors ordered him to keep silent, to avoid speaking about his beliefs, to stop singing. He replied, "What would a nightingale do if ordered to stop singing? It cannot stop, and neither can I."

So they tortured him and in the end drowned him after stabbing him repeatedly in the heart.

While under persecution, he sent word to his
mother: "They give me much pain. I might die at
their hands. But don't weep, mother. [He was
twenty-one. At that age it is still possible to believe
you can stop a mother from weeping.] An angel
showed me heavenly Jerusalem, and it is beautiful.
Do your best, mother, to meet me there."

Did this Vania really see an angel? People can
have foolish hallucinations. But we have proof he
did, because, as an uncultured peasant boy, he
described this angel as no professor of theology
would.

He went on to say, "Angels are transparent. When
you have one in front of you and a man stands
behind him, the presence of the angel does not keep
you from seeing the man. On the contrary, you see
him better. Seen through an angel, all men look
more lovely. You can understand and appreciate
even a torturer."

Many regret they have never looked upon an
angel. They are wrong. You see an angel as often as
you accept an unlovely person, as often as you love
the one who hurts you.

Vania Moiseev is the pride of our Romanian
nation.

Another is the young girl Sophia Chiriac. From
the age of eighteen she worked in the underground
print shop of the unregistered Soviet Baptists.
Confined in a small cellar full of machines, paper,
ink, and stocks of books, she had little room to
move, stagnant air to breathe, and never any sun-
shine. She became sick but could not go to a
physician. The rule of conspiracy is that once on the
staff of such a secret enterprise you never leave it till

near death. When she was finally taken to a hospital, it was too late. Sophia was a Romanian girl who had sacrificed her life to give light to the Russian nation that had subjugated her own.

And then there is another Bessarabian, the well-known confessor Nikolai Horev, who was repeatedly in Soviet jails and came out each time strengthened in faith, a shining example to others. From all he said and wrote, I value most a prayer of his: "Lord, you are my shepherd forever, and I am your sheep forever. May your rod always be in your hand so that when I am in danger, you will protect me from my enemies, or when I stray from your way into wrong paths, either through temptation or through the fear of difficulties, you will use your rod to bring me back to the right way. And should I ever ask you, O Lord, for anything different from what I am asking you now, please ignore it."

Have you ever asked God to ignore your prayers if they should keep you, or others through you, from becoming a saint?

We hope Bessarabia, as well as all the other territories formerly belonging to Romania, will soon unite with the motherland. At this moment, the fact that we have a Communist government bodes ill for the fulfillment of our national ideal: the union of all Romanians.

Confessions

Much of my time in Romania was taken up with hearing confessions.

I was terribly tired after having preached twice or thrice a day, but was not allowed to go to bed. Some with burdened hearts asked me to listen to them.

Perhaps it is good for confessors to be tired, because then they speak less and don't interrupt, letting the words and tears of the penitents just flow.

Not one of the main collaborators with the Communists and none of the outright traitors confessed this particular sin. I met with men who had denounced their brethren in faith to the authorities, knowing how much they would have to suffer as a result. When I was arrested, the police officer who interrogated me let slip the name of one who had denounced me. In another case, I was given the actual denunciation to read. Those guilty of such extremes of apostasy never confessed the worst they had done. They told of sins that were minimal, but their disproportionate regret showed that they carried a much heavier, though unacknowledged, burden.

I understood. Cain, after killing his brother, said to God, "*Gadol avoni linso*—My sin is greater than one can bear" (Gen. 4:13).

When conscience reproaches a person for an extreme sin, memory tells him, "You never did it." And memory usually succeeds in convincing conscience. This happened in Germany. It was too difficult to acknowledge that millions of Jews had been killed, so conscience was silenced. Memory won: "It did not happen."

I know how difficult it is for me to admit the worst sins I have committed and my reluctance to confess them to anyone, even to God. On the other hand, reason tells me—very often rightly—that it is far from wise for a person with standing in the church to tell his sins to any man. An American evangelist produced havoc for the babes in Christ by confessing on TV, before an audience of millions, a sin that only two or three persons knew about.

In Romania we had an Orthodox monk, Arsene Boca, who would tell the penitent, "I know it is too difficult for you to relate certain things you did. Therefore I will tell them to you." He was a man with clairvoyance. But a confessor doesn't need this quality. It can drive one mad to know all the sins of his interlocutors. Be modest. Be happy about the little you are told. God is a modest God. David and Manasseh did not spell out all the gruesome details of their sins. David simply said to Nathan, "I have sinned against the Lord" (2 Sam. 12:13). No more was required.

However, the brethren who have sinned most profoundly under Communism did not confess, though some of them might have made decisions in their heart to change. You may wonder who confessed with tears: it was the best, the most heroic. They felt guilty, some for having survived. If they had been heroic the whole time—and no one could have been—if they had stepped forward and protested each time another was beaten, they would have died of the many beatings they would have received.

Others felt guilty that, because of their involvement in the underground church, the family had broken up. Their children had not approved of the fact that father or mother went to jail for their beliefs and left them to eat from the garbage, suffer poor health, and forego proper schooling. Their reproach was always the same: "If father had kept quiet like so many other believers, we would not have been deprived of a normal childhood." And so the parent returned from jail and found hostile children and

sometimes a bitter spouse, too. They felt it was all
their fault.

It is difficult to win in this life. Other children
were rebellious against parents who had played a
treacherous role. These children could not bear the
thought of being children of a Judas. Many felt
guilty for having lied to the police during investigation, to protect themselves or to keep others from
being arrested. They had been taught strict honesty.
For Christians who think like this, it would have
been wise never to engage in secret work. Such
work is impossible for someone who considers it a
sacred principle always to tell the full truth. A Bible
smuggler from the West to Eastern Europe told me,
"I never said a lie." I asked him, "When applying for
a Russian or Romanian visa, what did you declare as
the purpose of your visit?" He replied, "Tourism."
This was a lie.

"Lies" in self-defense, in defense of innocents or
the church, are not really lies. When in danger of
death, Paul defended himself before the priestly
council with these words: "I am a Pharisee, the son
of a Pharisee; concerning the hope and resurrection
of the dead I am being judged" (Acts 23:6), which
was certainly not the issue. But those who felt the
guilt of having lied were indifferent to any ethical
niceties. They said, "If these Communist police were
to find out that I lied to them in matters about which
I was questioned, how would they believe what I
told them about salvation?"

Others had something else on their heart. They
had not seen a female for years, even decades. Once
free, they found every girl an irresistible temptation.
(This was less true of Catholic priests, who had been

brought up with the discipline of celibacy, than of evangelicals.) I told everyone about the blood of Christ that cleanses every sin, and souls found rest. Such conversations in intimacy were as important as speeches delivered to audiences of thousands.

I had the advantage of having known great confessors personally. One was an English missionary to the Romanian Jews, David Adeney. When a person confessed a major sin to him, Adeney would weep. His tears spoke. He added to them not a word. I had also known the Lutheran bishop, Frederic Muller. No matter what sin of mine I told him, he would always reply, "This I have, too. It belongs to all men, just as forgiveness belongs to God."

I had known the Orthodox priest Suroianu who, when I told him many sins of mine, said, "Well, you have plenty of sins, and grievous ones. But beware of one sin, that of despair. Never believe that your sins can be more or greater than God's grace. You can never out-sin God. He forgives for Christ's sake. Go in peace."

The Brother Who Died for Me

To each person who came to me, sometimes four or five in an evening, I told a story that I had told to robbers and murderers in jail. I felt it was appropriate for saints carrying remorse, and I offer it to the reader for comfort, regardless of the monstrous sins he may have committed.

In the olden days there were two brothers, the elder good and devout, the younger a libertine who reveled with unsavory companions. The elder brother prayed for the younger and often begged him to change his life, but all seemed in vain.

One night as the elder brother sat in his study reading, the younger brother rushed into his room, begging, "Save me! The police are after me! I have killed a man." There were bloodstains on his clothes.

The older brother grasped the situation immediately and said, "I will save you. Let us change clothes." He took the bloodstained suit of the criminal and gave him his white robe.

The two had barely dressed when the police arrived. They had pursued the criminal from the place where the deed had been committed and seized the brother in the bloodstained garment.

Brought before the judge, he pleaded guilty, saying, "I bear the whole responsibility for the crime."

Faced with the evidence before him—the pursuit, the blood, the confession—the judge had no doubt. He sentenced the man to death, then asked him his final wish.

"Only one," said the supposed criminal. "I want my brother to receive this letter, which I have prepared for him, at the very moment I am hanged."

The wish was granted.

The next day, his brother received the letter. Opening it, he read: "My beloved, at this very moment, I die in your place, in your bloodstained clothes, for your crime—and I am happy to offer this sacrifice on your behalf.

"But I would like you, in the white clothes I gave you, to lead a life of righteousness and purity. I have no other desire!"

The younger brother, on reading these words, was taken by remorse. He ran to stop the execution—but it was too late. Then he ran to the judge to confess his crime, but the judge would not listen to him. "A murder was committed; it has been expiated. What was between you two brothers is of no interest to us."

After that, as often as his former comrades in revelry called the young lad to drinking parties and loose living, he would say, "In the white clothes left to me by the brother who gave his life for me, I can no longer do the evil deeds I did before."

You Received an Angel

I was in the Christian home of a couple I had married some forty years before. They reminded me of what I had preached at their wedding.

I had told them that on the preceding evening, unable to sleep, I was wondering what to say to them at the ceremony. My wife was already asleep. I was having considerable difficulty finding a suitable text for the occasion. Only one verse of the Bible kept coming to my mind: "Do not forget to entertain strangers, for by so doing some have unwittingly entertained angels" (Heb. 13:2). I dismissed it. How can one make a wedding sermon out of that?

But since it was on my mind, I tried to figure out who of the many who had stayed in our home was an angel. Some later proved to be devils, some were nice people, but angels? None fell into this category. While speculating like this, I chanced to look at my sleeping wife, and said to myself, "This is the angel entertained by me unwittingly." That became the text of my wedding sermon. "You, the bridegroom, are now receiving an angel. Angels were badly treated in Sodom. Others are not taken into consideration. You give to your bride the honor due to an angel."

Forty years have passed. He still calls her not by her name, but "angel."

In the USA, 50% of marriages end in divorce, and probably a good percentage of the other half are torn by quarrels. Even a great number of pastors divorce. I rejoice that it is not so in my homeland. Divorce among evangelicals is a rare event.

It would be easy to say that this situation is due to the greater spirituality among believers, but there is a more down-to-earth explanation: the hardship of life. When husband and wife, after a day of hard labor, have to stand in line many hours for the bare necessities of life, there is less time to quarrel. One man told me, "Our apartment is not heated in winter. The electricity bill is high. We cannot afford to have many bulbs burning. The cozy atmosphere needed for a good quarrel is missing, so we forego it."

In contrast to this, the opulence in the West favors divorce. I have known couples who divorced because of quarrels about how to squander their surplus on futilities. If western Christians gave more of their surplus to good causes, the number of divorces would drastically decrease.

Christianity and Communism

This leads me to express a few thoughts about the relationship between Christianity and Communism.

I have long been aware that, on a practical level, sinful mankind does not know a better economic system than capitalism. This system conflicts with Communism; between Christianity and Communism there is not a total contradiction. How is it that the name "Communism" is so much akin to notions dear to Christians, such as "the communion of saints," "holy communion," etc.? Whenever I met with a convinced revolutionary, I felt guilty. I would say to myself, "He is the wrong kind of Communist, because I am not the right kind."

Nowadays we discuss how one becomes a Christian: is it through infant or believer's baptism, sprinkling or immersion? Does one receive the Holy Spirit at the same time, or is this a second experience? Which denomination should one join, if any? It was not so in the beginning. In the early years of the Christian church, all believers "had all things in common, and sold their possessions and goods and divided them among all, as anyone had need" (Acts 2:44-45). Today it is difficult to guess which confession is the church that Christ willed. Is it the Catholic, Orthodox, Lutheran, Baptist, Pentecostal, Adventist? However, we can be sure that one church was organized as Jesus willed it. After the resurrection, he spent forty days with his disciples and surely must have told them what to do. He taught that the multitude of those who believe should be of one heart and one soul; that no one should say that anything he possessed was his own; that they should have all things in common (Acts 5:32). Measured by this standard, all today's Christian denominations are heresies.

It is obvious that contemporary Christianity, which numbers hundreds of millions on all continents, must have other life structures than those Christianity had when it numbered only a few thousand in Jerusalem, but the principle should remain the same. We should all be able to say,

"None of us lives to himself, and no one dies to himself" (Rom. 14:7).

A theoretician of the New Age movement read my book *Tortured for Christ*, in which I describe the heroic virtues of Christians in the underground church under Communism. Then he wrote, "If today's Christians in the West were like this, the New Age movement would not have arisen." I paraphrase him: "If we had been the right kind of Communists, we would not have the wrong kind of Communists opposing us."

Meanwhile, we should not deceive ourselves. The Communist ideal has lost some very important battles, but it is far from being defeated or extinguished. A fourth of mankind is still under Communist rule. China with 1.1 billion people and Russia with 280 million which still has a one-party Communist system at the moment I write these lines. There is Communism in Vietnam, Ethiopia, Zimbabwe, Angola, and Cuba. In Nicaragua, the army, police, and trade unions are still under Communist control, while the government belongs to a divided opposition.

And there are still thousands in Romania and other eastern countries, where a major change has taken place, who still want Communism—some to regain the privileges they lost, some because they retain their Communist ideology. Many of the political concepts they believed in, many axioms they took for granted, crumbled with the Berlin Wall, but they are still sure that a society in which people have all things in common and share according to need, a society without millionaires on one side and homeless on the other, is to be preferred to the capitalist society in which profit is the main-spring for action.

Is there any Christian who loves Jesus' teachings who does not see that they have a point? It might not be practical, but many impractical things have spiritual value. We should all feel some uneasiness in our conscience when we read the Master's words: "Sell all you have and give to the poor, if you wish to be perfect." Is there anyone among us who does not have a longing for perfection?

Our God is modest and looks at our modest, sincere desires as if they were accomplished facts. It is not easy to go back two thousand years and fulfill all commands literally just as they were given. But I feel a bond uniting me with every sincere Communist and can extend to him wholehearted love. The fact that I suffered under Communism is not sufficient motive to reject it totally.

Communists no longer kill wholesale in Russia or Romania, but they continue to kill retail wherever they have guerrillas, as in India, the Philippines, and Latin America. Though they are killers, they are also ready to die for their beliefs. Therefore, they should not be simply discarded as worthless junk. Communism is the old dream of mankind for a kingdom of justice and happiness. Whence did this ideal arise if not from a reminiscence of paradise? Many anthropologists maintain that Communism is the first primitive social order. Communism as practiced by Marxism has been and still is horrible. Today, even the Communist press in Russia admits this.

Distinguish Ideals from Their Supporters

Some will be shocked that I, a man who has suffered so much, can still say a good word about Communism as a principle. Intellectual and spiritual progress is impossible if we do not make a clear-cut distinction between an ideal that can be sublime and the gruesome deeds of those who proclaim themselves its adherents.

If we were to take into account the very base deeds committed at a certain stage of their lives by David, Solomon, and Paul, we would have to discard their writings as unacceptable.

Great crimes have been committed over the centuries against Jews and fellow Christians of other persuasions as well. Because of this, should we forego Christian teaching altogether? Christians love their enemies—all their enemies. They have a loving understanding for what makes a man an enemy. Communists, on the other hand, are passionate in evil. They have learned Communism from Marx, who had connections with Satanism, as I proved in my book *Marx—Prophet of Darkness*.

Christians can teach what the first Christians learned directly from Jesus: to have all things in common; not to claim anything for oneself; to share with the brethren. After two thousand years, living as we do under entirely different circumstances, we may not be able to follow this command explicitly. But the great principle remains: Christians have to deny themselves, deny their ego, their selfishness. Not one of us lives or dies to himself. Let us show that the spirit of primitive Christianity has not been extinguished.

I believe there is no greater and more effective Communism ever propagated in the world than the loving, giving Communism practiced by the first

Christians and continued by many groups since. It is the only solution for the economic and social ills of the world. Mankind will have to ascend a steep road toward this ideal. For the time being, however, capitalism is surely better than Communism as we have seen it.

Dancing in Prison

Once when I was especially hungry in the Jilava jail, Lieutenant Franco from the *Securitate* came to investigate me. Angry about such an untimely visit, I decided I would investigate him. I asked him about his soul, with the result that he was converted and gave me the lunch he had brought for himself: sandwiches with fine, white bread and the most expensive sausage. I even had dessert—luscious chocolate candies. He now lives in Israel.

Another time, in the solitary cell under what later became the headquarters of the Central Committee of the Communist Party, I remembered Jesus' words: "When men hate you and revile you, rejoice and leap for joy" (Luke 6:23). It occurred to me that I had neglected a duty. I had rejoiced but not leaped for joy, as Jesus had taught us to do. So I began to dance around the cell. The warden, who kept an eye on me through the peephole in the door, was sure I had gone mad. Guards had orders to behave well towards madmen so they would not disturb the silence of the prison. To quieten me down, he brought a large loaf of bread, cheese, and two pieces of sugar.

Romania should do what all believers are intended to do when in distress. Do nothing practical to remedy a situation that is irremediable. Just praise

the Lord, sing and dance in His honor. Angels can
take care of the rest, not only for individuals but also
for whole nations. Isaiah recommended just "quiet-
ness and confidence" (Isa. 30:15). Some will discard
such advice as foolishness. But surely it is more
practical to be a fool in Christ than to be a "wise"
man foolishly angry about what he cannot change.

Why No Apology?

In spontaneous actions, western evangelical and
Catholic groups have done much to help the
Romanian people in need since the revolution.
Great quantities of Bibles and good Christian books
have also been sent in.

But this is not enough to establish right relations
between East and West.

After the War, the churches of Germany,
acknowledging that Nazism killed millions of Jews,
made public statements of apology for having supported the Nazis or at least for allowing mass
slaughter to take place without protesting and helping the persecuted to escape. The German democratic government itself recognized their national guilt
and gave great sums of money in restitution to the
surviving victims.

Romania and other Eastern European states
were given into the hands of Communist butchers—
already known as such—by Britain and the USA at
Yalta. In his memoirs, Churchill says that he passed
a slip of paper to Stalin, whom he had characterized
previously as a bloody criminal, with the following
proposal: "You give me Greece and Romania will be
yours." He disposed of Romania as if it were his private possession. Roosevelt went along with him as

they committed their nations to handing over whole countries to God-hating rulers. Hundreds of thousands of innocents died as a result. My country has been ruined.

Until Vatican 2, the papacy was the only large religious body that took an anti-Communist stance and defended the persecuted. After Vatican 2, they gave up their crusade. Meanwhile, the World Council of Churches for thirty years has harshly criticized the western world while covering up the atrocities taking place in the East. It has vigorously supported liberation theology, which means liberation from capitalism but never from the injustices of Communism. The great Protestant bodies, such as Lutheran and Reformed World Federation, followed suit. During the worst years of terror, Romania was visited by bishops, pastors and renowned evangelists. Not one said a word in defense of the sufferers.

I was reminded of the fact that in 1935, when Hitler ruled Germany, the Baptist World Alliance chose Berlin as the location for its world congress. Hitler's program to exterminate the Jews was known. While the delegates quoted Bible verses written by Jews about the Jew Jesus and spoke about His sufferings, not one word of compassion or solidarity was spoken on behalf of the German Jews threatened with mass murder. There was only one American Jewish Christian among the delegates, a Mr. Gartenhaus, but he was not allowed to speak from the rostrum.

On one occasion, I read the report of an Anglican bishop in his diocesan bulletin about his visit to Romania. He wrote glowingly about the many lavish breakfasts (wrongly so-called, because they broke no fasts), luncheons, and dinners, but said nothing about the Christians starving in jail.

Today foreign church leaders are certainly welcome in Romania, but it would be appropriate for them to express some word of repentance. They might also publicly acknowledge that during the years of terror not one denomination had budgeted so much as one pound for the families of Christian martyrs, who never received one parcel of food from abroad. On the other hand, through the World Council of Churches, many denominations have given money to Communist guerrillas in Africa who, when they came to power, imprisoned and killed Christians. Mozambique and Angola are prime examples. Again, no money ever went to families of prisoners.

Teach, but Also Learn

Something else needs to be said about the relationship of the West with Romanian churches (and also for other countries of the former eastern bloc).

Western Christians can afford the luxury of expensive journeys to teach others. Why then don't they invite Romanian or Russian Christians to evangelize in the West? Why, at large evangelistic congresses, are only well-fed, affluent western evangelists the key speakers? It was not so in the early church. There, men like Paul shared the mysteries of Christ learned while in chains.

Hands that have worn chains can give blessings and should be awarded this privilege. In the first centuries, the church in Rome was heeded by others because it had given the most martyrs.

One more detail: in Romanian evangelical

churches women use no makeup and wear no jewelry. Believers who do so are not accepted as church members. Smoking and drinking are strictly forbidden. American evangelists who wear rings and whose wives use lipstick are not acceptable.

It is helpful to know this.

The Duty to Howl

Many western preachers have had the advantage of a theological education, which can be very profitable. Many of the Romanian preachers, as well as Russian, Bulgarian, etc., have not been in seminaries but in dark cells, hungry, beaten, and suffering with the cold.

I cannot explain why, but in certain cells in utter cold and darkness, prisoners could not refrain from howling. God says, "I will howl for Moab" (Jer. 48:31). Before being in such a cell, I had never imagined how terrible is God's pain for sinners. It makes Him howl. I now knew another aspect of God: a God who howls. This is also a revelation about Him.

It can be learned best from those who have been through this school. They have fulfilled an amazing commandment from God: "Howl for Babylon." Howl for the worst enemy of your people. We howled in these cells for our Communist torturers, knowing that if we did so, "they may be healed" (Jer. 51:8). We consider it important that a minister should be trained in homiletics, dogmatics, Greek, Hebrew, and church history. The West can give us teachers for these. But ministers must also be prepared for howling, for being men who feel they will die if souls are not saved.

The prophet Joel says, "Howl, all you who minister before the altar" (Jer. 1:13). Preachers should imitate Micah, who at a given moment made the decision, "I will wail and howl" (Micah 1:8), not, "I will preach according to the rules of rhetoric."

Perhaps eastern preachers can teach the West how to weep when you have been stabbed with the knife of treason, how to bear the burden of suffering for the honor and good of the holy church. They will add that the great suffering is not produced by lost battles (no warrior can win them all) or by physical wounds, but by brothers and sisters who do not take up a cross and fight the good fight, who renounce the holy dream. They will teach us to smile not only when comforted by friends, with lilies strewn in their path, but also when surrounded by enemies, with nails driven into their bodies.

A Heavenly Smile

Speaking of smiles, let me write about one fellow-prisoner whom I did not meet again on Romanian soil because he is now in a better land.

We usually imagine the saints as being in a heaven far away. The Bible tells us in Hebrews 12:1 that they surround us. They continue to be interested in all they left behind and participate in the fight. They inspire us in the very strict sense of the word.

It is said about a disciple of John Chrysostom, the greatest preacher Christianity has ever had, that he peered into the room where his master was preparing a sermon and saw two unknown beings whispering something in his ears. Curious, he asked about them and received this reply: "It was wrong of you to peek, but since you did, I will tell you. These were the apostles Paul and John, who sometimes suggest what I should preach about."

This story might be legend, but the fact remains that we are in the communion of the saints of all times. It is good for those who visit Romania not only to look around to see living saints, but also to look up and through the spirit get a glimpse of those in glory who surround them.

I remembered Milan Haimovici, a Hebrew Christian pastor who spent seven years in jail. Even enemies of both Jews and the gospel admired his courage. He would protest against any injustice on the part of the wardens though he knew that for this he would be savagely beaten.

Once I was in a large cell holding perhaps a hundred prisoners. We were crammed together in utter misery with no room to walk even a few steps. We were over come with the dirt and the stench. At night it was impossible to sleep because there were always three or four who snored, each on a different melody. When they stopped others started. Some coughed, some sneezed, some quarreled.

In these close quarters were Christians of many denominations, Jews, atheists, men of all political parties and social categories. Among them was Milan, who witnessed for Jesus. He had no Bible and had seen no book for many years. He could advance no intellectual arguments. He could only say repeatedly, "I know Jesus. Walk and talk with Him."

A professor, member of the Royal Academy of Sciences, scoffed: "Jesus has been dead for two thousand years. How can you talk with Him? Even admitting that He was resurrected, as you Christians believe, and went to heaven, this heaven is millions of miles away. Don't tell us any more lies. No one can walk and talk with Him."

Milan simply repeated, "I wonder myself how it can happen and have no real explanation, but it is a fact. He walks and talks with me." A great circle of prisoners listened to the discussion. Continuing, Milan asserted, "I even see Him sometimes."

This was too much for a man of science. "What you say is the greatest lie I have heard in all my life. Since you claim you see Him, can you please tell us how He looks at you: angry, wrathful, bored, indifferent, polite, interested, loving? Does He perhaps also smile at you?"

Milan replied, "How did you guess that? Really, He sometimes smiles at me."

"Well, well," said the professor. "You are lucky I am not a psychiatrist, or I would diagnose you as having religious mania. Perhaps you can show us how Jesus smiles."

"I will gladly try," said Milan.

The scene that followed was the most beautiful in the eighty-one years of my life. Like all the rest of us, Milan resembled a scarecrow. Shorn, dirty, with dark circles around his eyes; only skin and bones, with teeth missing, and in a zebra uniform, he was anything but attractive. But when he received this challenge, his face began to shine—the glory of God can shine through a thick crust of dirt—and a beautiful smile appeared on his lips. Romeo must have looked like this when he smiled at Juliet.

There was a touch of sadness in the smile because of the lost condition of his questioner's soul. But one could read on his lips a passionate love, an unquenchable longing, a sure hope and an ardent desire of a lover to receive the kiss of the beloved. All the splendor of heaven was in this magnificent smile. (An ugly thought passed through my mind on seeing this smile: the definition of the word "kiss" in a Russian dictionary—"the mutual touch of two pairs of lips with reciprocal transmission of microbes and carbon dioxide." Who can avoid such wrong thoughts at a sublime moment?) The atheist professor bowed his head and said, "Sir, you have seen Jesus."

When I became a Christian, I was advised to read every day a page from the Bible and the life of a saint, a martyr, or a renowned missionary, which I do. But before I was in jail, I read the lives of saints with skepticism. The writers always seemed to exaggerate. I knew the story of the charming and convincing smile of Bernadette de Soubiroux of Lourdes. I had known several Christians on earth who had heavenly smiles (one of whom is my wife Sabina). But now I saw such smiles in conditions of utter suffering.

I have seen them many times, in many jails. Sometimes I have difficulty remembering the circumstances. All the great smilers became one for me, fusing into the smile of Jesus. Saints bring the smile of heaven into the deepest valleys of the shadow of death. Men with such a smile do not die. They surround us after death as well, encouraging and helping us. Romania has just such a cloud of witnesses above it. This too is a Romanian reality. A Christian who goes to such a place must look for it.

A renowned church leader told me that he had visited Lenin's tomb in Moscow and had seen his mummy. I asked him if he had perceived the presence of some other dead person in Russia. He had not. But Paul says in Hebrews 13:1 that he had seen a cloud of God's witnesses from thousands of years before.

Killed for Distributing Bibles

Milan Haimovici is one of many martyrs who beautify the sky over Romania. I am very much attached to some of them because in a certain sense I played a role in their dying under tragic circumstances.

We know the names of four Romanian Christians who had to die for the crime of distributing Bibles they had received from us through underground channels. Clipa was caught and badly tortured to reveal how he obtained and distributed the Bibles. Then he was found hanged. No one really knows how he died. Did the Communists hang him? Did he commit suicide, like many others in Communist China, fearing he might weaken and betray when subjected to further torture? Another Bible distributor, Bogdam, was also found hanged. Tudose was found electrocuted. Pastor Radu Cruceru died of a staged automobile accident, a method of killing much practiced by the Communists.

If we and others from abroad had not smuggled in Bibles, these persons would have lived. We bear a responsibility that their wives are widows and their children orphans. Every Christian who contributes to such a work should know that someone at the receiving end might give blood in the cause for which we in the free world give money.

Some do this underground work in Communist

and Muslim countries without pangs of conscience. But I know directors, personnel, and supporters of our mission who are very conscious of the risks and suffer because of it. They feel it is not enough to give money and send Bibles; we must share with those in Communist countries the pain, the tears, and the sorrows of the distributors and their families. Some dear saints in the West have broken down mentally under this burden. It gives me many sleepless nights. Couriers of our mission have been killed in China, too. And some were imprisoned for many years under the appalling conditions of Communist jails, among them the translator of my book *Tortured for Christ* into the Amharic language of Ethiopia.

Don't Give Money Easily

I was scheduled to preach at a large meeting in Norway that was called for the special purpose of gathering money for Ukrainian Bibles. The mission counted on my presence to be an encouragement to others to give more.

I told the crowd the story of Nikolai Hmara, a Soviet Christian who had died for Christ after having his tongue cut off and his eyes gouged out, and I ended by saying, "Don't be quick to give. You might be punished by God for having given money to print Ukrainian Bibles. Some will believe so devoutly that the Bible you donate is the word of God that they will be ready to endure prison, torture and death for sharing it. Your Bibles will be read in the Soviet Ukraine, where those who read the word will follow its command and renounce everything for the sake of the kingdom. Some will prefer

Jesus to wife, mother, and children, and will fulfill dangerous tasks in the underground church, such as working in secret print shops or running forbidden Sunday schools. If they are caught, their wives might remain widows and their children orphans, who may later accuse their father of putting religion above duty to provide daily bread for the family.

"The Bible you donate might inspire someone else to become a Nikolai Hmara. You will answer to God for having given this money if your life does not show that you yourself obey the Bible as the word of God, if you do not lead a life of intimacy with Jesus, following Him on the way of the cross, of prayer and praise and self-sacrifice.

"If you do not intend to commit yourselves wholeheartedly to Jesus, it is best for you not to give. Please forego giving."

It remains for the reader of these lines to guess whether the offering on that evening was large or small.

I constantly hear the cries of those suffering in Communist countries because they desire the spreading of the gospel and relief for their abandoned families. This spurs me on when I feel my age and feel tempted to give up. But Bishop Meshkala died in Albania at the age of eighty-four after forty-three years in jail! He was not too old to suffer for Christ and never gave up. Should I give up my fight under entirely different circumstances?

Some, after reading this book, might feel like giving money for the cause of Christians in Communist countries or in those only recently liberated. Giving will oblige you to have fellowship with them in their heavy tribulations. Think carefully about what you intend to do.

Loving the Enemy

Every place I visited in Romania brought back other memories to my mind.

In Bucharest, I preached in the Dragosh Voda Brethren church. This building had been used before by my church in its peregrinations from one place to another under different dictatorships.

It was immediately after the invasion of Romania by Soviet troops toward the end of the Second World War. Whole units of the German army that had occupied our country were taken captive. They had no illusions. Slavery in Siberia would be their lot. For many it would mean death. While a large group of German prisoners of war were being led to their barracks, two officers succeeded in escaping from the surveillance of the escort. Still wearing their Nazi uniforms, they wandered trembling through the streets of Bucharest. The one thing that shielded them was the night. We were still at war, and the streets were only very dimly lit.

All at once they spotted a ray of hope: a sign saying "Lutheran Chapel." They knew the Lutherans of Romania to be of German extraction. Here someone would help them. What a disappointment awaited them when they heard that we were Jewish! Jews had more reason to hate the German soldiers than even the Soviets did.

I quieted their fears. "We are Jews, but also Christians and give no one into the hands of their enemies. There is a story about a lamb led to slaughter that fled and ran to Moses, asking him to protect it. He replied, "I cannot do so. God has ordained that your meat should serve as food for men," and he handed the lamb to the butcher. A Jewish writing says that God hid His face for shame at what a man who bore His name could do.

"We have suffered under the German occupation. But you personally may not be guilty. In any case, we are not your judges. You are welcome in our home. We will also give you civilian clothes so that you can try to make your way to Germany."

We were then under a decree forbidding anyone to hide a German soldier under pain of death. In time this developed into a systematic work of helping persecuted Germans just as, during the war, we had used our influence in Christian circles to help persecuted Jews.

The believers in the Brethren church where I was now asked to preach knew all this. They knew that I meant it when I spoke about forgiving those who have abused you, even the God-hating Communists.

So I traveled from one place to another in Bucharest and then to different cities and towns, reliving events of the past.

Revisiting Places where I Sinned

I not only saw places that held pleasant or sacred memories, but also places where I had gravely sinned.

I saw once again the homes in which my family had lived when I was young. I had been very evil towards a mother who had sacrificed herself for her orphaned children.

Here was the quarter called—I don't know

why—"The Stone Cross." It was a place of prostitution. "Friends" led me here when I was twelve. No Christian stood before the ill-famed house warning youngsters not to enter. The first time I saw the half-naked women, I fled. Not so the second time. I saw again the places where I had taken advantage of other women. I saw gambling houses that I had frequented, places where I had met with other blasphemers and mocked God, places where I had failed and sinned even as a Christian and then a pastor.

I had confessed this whole life of sin and believed that Christ had forgiven everything. Paul wrote that he pressed forward, forgetting those things that were behind him. But he, too, could not forget his whole past. He tells us about it. Neither could I forget it all.

In Romania I thought, too, of all the shortcomings and grave sins committed during the quarter of a century lived abroad.

How happy I was that "there is a fountain filled wit blood drawn from Emmanuel's veins" and that if one plunged into this fountain, a great miracle takes place. Not only are sins (even crimes) forgiven, but they become white as snow. They become visible tokens of actual purity. What happens to them is beyond description. Jesus was made sin. One of the purposes was to show what beauties can be made of sins through repentance, as a potter can make a luxurious vase out of what had been mud.

However, like the pieces of pottery or like metal that has to be refined, we must pass through the fires of affliction. This cleansing process lasts until all impurity has disappeared, which in our case means until all complaining, all rebellion, all pestering God with the question "Why?," all selfishness, pride, and an unreadiness to forgive have disappeared.

A little girl watched a goldsmith hold the costly metal in a jar for purifying. Repeatedly he took out the slack and the metal shone more and more beautifully. The girl asked, "How long does this go on?" He said, "Have patience." The goldsmith had to repeat the words often as he waited for the moment called "the silver look," when he saw his image in the metal.

This is how the heavenly Goldsmith works. A sinner who has passed through His purification has a beauty he never had before, the beauty of Christ Himself.

Encounter with a Top Soviet Official

For twenty-five years I have played in the world the role of Tychicus (Eph. 6:21), who during Paul's day made known to the brethren how the persecuted were doing. While in Romania, I had the opposite role: to tell how the church in the free world is faring, as well as how we worked for the persecuted while they were under the yoke of Communism.

Romanian Christians were aware of the fact that Bibles and other books entered their country, along with financial aid and radio broadcasts, but they did not know about the vast organizations that were behind all this and about the thousands upon thousands of fellow believers who gave sacrificially and prayed for them. They were most interested in our Christian Mission to the Communist World and its work in over forty countries. I told them not only about the relief work for the persecuted but also about our missionary endeavors among their persecutors. I will mention here just one of my most interesting experiences in this area.

In Switzerland, another brother and I visited a world industrial exhibition. The most beautiful section was the Soviet department, the only one to add a fashion show, which attracted thousands, and a religious exhibit which was very well put together.

At the entrance was a huge picture of Billy Graham preaching in Moscow, of the Patriarchy, and of the one single synagogue in Moscow, a city with 200,000 Jews, of a mosque, and so on. The obvious aim was to reveal the perfect religious freedom that exists under Communism.

An album was prepared for each visitor to register his impressions.

I wrote the following: "I congratulate you for this unique idea to ornament an industrial exposition with words and pictures about religion. If there were no God, there would be no human mind and no industry. Everything you show is well arranged, but as a friend of the USSR, I would suggest that you enrich this exposition with other valorous pictures: that of Nikolai Hmara, a Baptist who, because of his faith, had his tongue cut off and his eyes gouged out. I can provide you with the picture of his corpse. The picture of Nikolai Hrapov would fit well, too. He spent thirty-four years in jail for his faith. Also that of Vania Moiseev, stabbed seven times in the region of his heart and then drowned," and so on and on.

A gentleman I believed to be from the Soviet staff read what I wrote and said, "There is a wicked man by the name of Wurmbrand who spreads such slander about us." After I told him I was that very same Wurmbrand, we spoke with each other for four hours. He was the head of the Foreign Department of their Ministry of Cults, a top man of the Soviet government on religious matters. He spoke fluent English and German. He had read all my books as well as other publications of our mission.

He started in a bellicose manner by saying there is no persecution. I answered, "It would be useless to contradict you, because you are obliged to speak thus. Let us rather pass to something much more important.

"A day will come when you will no longer be a man in high position in the Communist Party and government, and I will no longer be a pastor. We will both die. For a short time someone who loves us will weep at our grave. Then those who knew us will die too, and we will lie in a forgotten grave.

"What happens after that? If at this point everything is ended, then it is stupid to be a Christian pastor and just as stupid to be an atheist opponent of religion. The best course is to eat, drink, and have some amusement; nothing more. In my homeland of Romania, there was a custom in the olden days to give a person sentenced to death a good meal with all his favorite dishes before his execution. The accused ate and drank well, and then he was shot. If everything ends with death, the most beautiful life that Communism or capitalism can provide is no more than a henchman's meal. It would not be worth while to fight for any cause."

He listened without interrupting.

I told him that in my youth I was meditative and inclined to melancholy. I had had a bitter childhood, without any such childish pleasures as toys or chocolate. When other children in school ate chocolate, I would lick the wrapping paper because it smelled good.

"I was sure that a God could not exist. If he did, he would have given me a nicer childhood. But for some reason I liked to take lonely walks through cemeteries and read the inscriptions on gravestones. I do so even now. It makes for highly interesting reading. This person had been a general, and he died. Another was a renowned poet, and he died. Another was a banker, another a beggar. But the end of life was death.

"On every gravestone there were two figures, the year of birth and the year of death, with a stroke in between. This is the sign that nature draws over every life: a stroke. Thus life is annulled. Without knowing a thing about any religion, I said to myself at that time, 'I wish to find Someone who can give youth without old age and life without death.' It took me a long time, but I finally found this Someone."

He continued to absorb my words without interruption. He had a soul hungry for God. I told him how I had prayed the prayer of an atheist: "God, I know for sure you don't exist. But if you exist—and this I contest—it is not my duty to believe in you. It is your duty to reveal yourself to me. I regret that you do not exist. I could have wished that somewhere in this universe there should beat a heart of love. I speak as a madman to the nonexistent. Well, that is all."

I went on: "This prayer was accepted. God sent a carpenter my way, who told my wife and me the story of the Carpenter of Nazareth who lived and died for us and was resurrected."

He asked question after question. At the end of four hours, he said, "I must admit there are two problems to which we Marxists have no answers. First, how is it that something exists? We explain everything by evolution, but how come evolution exists and that the first living cell existed from which all animals, the monkey, and man came into being? Secondly, what happens to man after death? We have no answers; you have. Therefore you are strong and we are weak."

Later he played a role in liberalizing the Soviet policy towards religion, which in turn had an effect on Romania and the other Eastern European countries.

Our mission sees to it that specific Christian literature for Communists, such as my books *Answer to Moscow's Bible* and *Marx—Prophet of Darkness*, gets into their hands and those of their leaders, with amazing results. These books have been translated into many languages and distributed in Romania, Russia, China, Czechoslovakia, Poland, Ethiopia, Mozambique, and Angola, among others. The professor of atheism at the highest school of the Romanian Communist Party was converted through their ministry, along with many others in a number of Communist countries.

A Country Reduced to Poverty

Back in Bucharest I was driven around and I also walked the streets, but it was no more the same city. In times past it had been called "the Paris of the East" because of its beauty, but it had long since foregone its proud boast. The impression was one of hopelessness.

Grand avenues such as grace the largest western cities lie unfinished; they end in nothing. Ceaushescu had the sickness of gigantomania. All his enterprises were to be unsurpassed in greatness, but he could never finish what he began. Most houses are decayed. They were in ruins before the windows were put in. You can see the results of the ravaging earthquakes of the recent past, but also of the bloody unrest. Facades are blackened by fire, and in the walls are bullet holes.

The shops are empty. Long lines of people wait for hours in the hope, often vain, that there will be something to buy. The queues for bread begin at four in the morning. By seven there is no more bread. The black market flourishes. There you can buy strawberries, furs and shirts, or suspect alcoholic beverages made with chemicals that have killed many people.

Small children beg. Crime is rampant. Tourists are advised not to walk at night carrying money. The economy is in a coma and the populace lacks even basic necessities. Skyrocketing unemployment seems unavoidable. The USA and the European community have stopped giving aid because Communists are still in power. The present regime is unhappy, but the rulers continue to live well. In fact, Ceaushescu would be pleased with his successor, who has also killed innocents, just like his predecessor.

Although Communists are still in power in Romania, they are politically bankrupt, reduced to the level of a theatrical prop, just as in Russia.

The Danger of Commentaries

God declared "I am what I am, not what men

believe me to be." He is the entirely Other. We cannot fathom His ways.

Innumerable books have been written explaining how biblical prophecies correspond to current events. Many books were full of predictions about how the Communist colossus in the north, Russia, would attack Israel. Then the much-dreaded Battle of Armageddon would ensue, along with the reign of the Antichrist.

Some said that Kissinger was the Antichrist. Before these, others had offered biblical proof that Stalin, Hitler, and Mussolini were the Antichrist. Now a book denounces Gorbachev as this enigmatic person, especially since he is marked with an indisputable sign: a red spot on his forehead.

To one such writer I said, "Every book on prophecy written till now has proved to be false after twenty years." He did not mind.

When my twelve-year-old grandson Alex was with me at a Christian booksellers" convention recently, he saw a great deal of advertising for Bible commentaries. "What's a commentary?" he asked. I responded that there are many things in the Bible that are difficult to understand, for example, predictions of doom and great suffering that will arise in the latter days. These are explained in the commentaries.

His reply was, "Such predictions should not be explained but contradicted. Abraham did not write a commentary on God's prediction that Sodom would be destroyed, nor did Moses on the prediction that God would destroy the Jewish people. Instead, they pleaded with God that it should not take place, and they changed His mind. Why shouldn't we do the same instead of writing commentaries?"

The Power to Overturn Communism

God is not bound by what men say who are not commissioned to write or speak in His name. He has destroyed a great deal of the power of Communism and will destroy the rest, not through political events, but through the prayers of the saints and the power of the Word distributed under duress.

He altered the mind of Gorbachev and many of his comrades. They in turn destroyed the power of Communism as no bombs or political action could have done. No plagues from above were needed. Men can forestall tribulations even if predicted in the Bible. God foretold Nineveh's destruction but then relented from this decision. His love is more reliable than any word spoken or written in His name.

When God has shed His love in our hearts, we have enormous power. We can affect God. Zephaniah 3:17 says that we can make God rejoice with singing. Our burning love can change men, too. They can be consciously won by it. Others will be confused by the rays of our spirit and will lose the capacity to oppose us. The sun shines on some and gives them life; it burns others. So love is always effective regardless of whom it touches. Humans do not realize what enormous power they possess. It extends not only to the whole earth but also to the cosmos.

Daniel 8 tells about a king who cast down some of the host of heaven, exalted himself as high as the Prince of hosts, and cast truth down to the earth. A very great power of evil can exist in a man. But at

least this much power exists in good and saintly men
and women.

The church of Christ can finish with
Communism, with fanatical Islam, with the darkness
of heathenism, with a Judaism without the King of
the Jews.

I have many more things to say about my visits to
Romania after twenty-five years of enforced exile.
But I will permit myself to imitate Paul when he
said, "Time would fail me to tell of Gideon and
Barak and Samson and Jephthah, also of David and
Samuel and the prophets" (Heb. 11:32).

Strange Communion Services

Pastor Vasile Vadan's church in Bistritza was
destroyed with bulldozers. Treacherous official
Baptist leaders connived in this act. In a heavy frost,
he gave Communion to his flock on the ruins. The
surface of the wine was frozen. After preaching in
the open, he fell gravely ill of pneumonia, but that
did not prevent the Communists from putting him in
jail.

Many Communion services in Romania have
been strange. In home churches there would be
bread and wine on the table, but also a pot of tea and
biscuits in reserve. When a guest appeared unex-
pectedly, a person known as a Christian but sus-
pected as an informer, the wine would disappear
from the table in a second. The pot of tea and biscuits gave the impression that the meeting was just
a social gathering.

In jail there were times when we had no bread
and certainly no wine. We took Communion with
nothing, remembering how precious a thing "noth-

ing" was. The world was created out of nothing. The earth is suspended on nothing. Paul wrote that he was nothing. We learned to appreciate the value of nothing.

To write about all the beautiful things that can be said about Romania today and its church would fill a large volume. But I would like to say a few words about what our Christian Mission to the Communist World is doing in other parts of the world.

A Great Communist Strategem

When I left Romania, I thought that I would work only for my own country, but then the Rev. Stuart Harris, director of the European Mission, offered me a larger sphere: the whole of Europe. However, Communism stretches to all continents. And so we enlarged our vision to include the whole Communist world, though I never forgot Romania. [When I say "we," I mean all the co-founders of our international mission: the Rev. Stuart Harris (UK); Myrus Knutson and Casus Styrdy (USA); J. Maris (Holland); Hans Braun (Germany); H. Zürcher and Hedi Fluri (Switzerland); Pat Henegan (S. Africa); Laiso (Italy); Colette Grarsu (France); Reg Werry (Australia); and many, many others.]

We confront Communism as a whole, of which Romania is only a small part. The whole is affected by any one of the parts. What is happening in Communism today? We have seen great changes. Are they for real?

The changes in the USSR and Eastern Europe are real enough and concern politics, economics, even religion, all institutions that can be controlled. But there is no change in the attitude towards God or in the basic outlook on life. In his speech on the Seventieth Anniversary of the Bolshevik revolution, Gorbachev said, "We are moving towards a new world, the world of Communism. We shall never turn off that road." He repeated, with the same vigor, that he remains an atheist. If there is one thing we can learn from the Communists, it is consistency. They abide by their teachings.

At the end of the Second World War, the Communists were granted dominion over all of Eastern Europe, without firing a shot. Roosevelt and Churchill ceded them this hegemony at the Yalta conference because they promised free elections, which of course never occurred. They had won through deceit.

The bloody dictator Stalin, whom the Soviet press now accuses of having killed fifty million innocents, had made a tremendous impression on western rulers. After meeting him, an American diplomat commented, "His brown eyes are exceedingly wise and gentle. A child would like to sit on his lap and a dog would sidle up to him." Nothing has changed. After meeting Gorbachev, even a world-renowned evangelist praised his charm and his "warm eyes." But Gromyko, former president of the USSR, had recommended Gorbachev as successor with the words, "He can smile beautifully, but he also has steel teeth for biting."

Marx said, "Religion is the opiate of the people," which means it must be countered as resolutely as drugs. Lenin wrote, "Thousands of epidemics and natural catastrophes are to be preferred to the slightest notion of a god." Marx wrote in his poem

"The Player" that "hellish vapors" filled his brain and that he "bought a sword from the Prince of Darkness." (Elements of satanic rituals.) Communism continues to brandish this sword against religion.

God-haters are also haters of mankind. In a letter to Engels on the 18th of June, 1882, Marx called mankind "a bunch of rascals" who can "kiss my [obscenity]." But miracle of miracles, the party he created, which never renounced its militant atheism, has now reopened hundreds of churches and closes its eyes to intense religious activity. Today there is mass evangelism, Sunday school for children, and charitable work—all totally proscribed a short time ago. There are even processions on the street in which these words are sung: "For the Czar [title of Russian emperors], for our country and faith." Bibles and other Christian literature continue to enter freely. We have 100,000 letters from the USSR alone, thanking us for the literature individually received.

Communism is far from being defeated, but it has received mortal wounds. The Berlin Wall and the Iron Curtain crumble!

Communists have killed millions of believers, and they were sure religion was dying. Now the church triumphs. It is Communism that struggles for survival in Eastern Europe. There is no human explanation for these events. Thanks be to God for working this miracle!

When we began our mission twenty-four years ago, anti-Communists thought that Communism could be defeated only through war. They said, "Only a dead Communist is a good Communist."

We came with a new message: just as Communists subvert the free world with their poisonous doctrine, let us subvert them with the Gospel. Let us work secretly to make Christ known. Let us help the underground churches. Though the Communists hate us, let us win them with love. Let us pray for them and bring them to Christ.

I ended my book *Answer to Moscow's Bible* by calling upon the Reds to repent and confess their crimes openly. The Soviet press now acknowledges that their Party has killed tens of millions of innocents, and Gorbachev has apologized to the Patriarch. Articles by atheist lecturers and officers of their Secret Police appear, acknowledging that they have lied to the people and shed innocent blood. Yet many Communists still stick to their ideology, modified by what they call "glasnost" and "perestroika."

Glasnost and Perestroika

What is the secret behind these words? We fear it is another example of Communist deceit, a maneuver intended to lull the West to sleep. Terror could not uproot religion—the blood of the martyrs has always been the seed of the church—so the Communists are trying another approach.

In an article in *Kommunist*, Lunacharsky, author of *Socialism and Religion*, is quoted as predicting that persecution of religion would be counterproductive. (After seventy years of terror, 70% of adults are still believers.) He advocated that Communists create a "religion without God," a "religious atheism."

"Let the Christians believe," the argument runs.

"Communists will infiltrate Christian ranks, will befriend them, disguising themselves as having similar ideals on many points. They will attract Christians to common social actions and will influence them to keep only an external form of religion, while becoming basically as godless as ourselves."

The same situation took place in the Roman Empire during the fourth century, under Constantine the Great. Ten emperors had slaughtered Christians. Constantine did an about-face, gave them full liberty, and made Christianity a state religion. Under him every baby was baptized and declared a Christian. Thus Christianity seemed to triumph—but it ceased to be truly Christian. The church leadership increasingly became a tool of the emperors.

In the USSR, the Orthodox patriarch Pimen cabled to Gorbachev, "We express deep thankfulness for your attention to the needs of believers and for all you do to reestablish the Leninist norms." (Lenin's norms included the killing of millions of Christians and the destruction of churches.) Kharchev, then head of the Religious Council of the Soviet government, declared, "Religion is penetrating socialism, not on foot but on wheels. And since power belongs to the Party, it is up to us to steer those wheels in one direction or another, according to our interests."

Few Soviet Christians are aware that Gorbachev and his kin follow the same Constantinian road. He wants to give liberty to the church, but to a church that will not be really Christian. It will be an outreach of Communism just as it had been of the Czar. Yeltsin asserts he is converted, but in his government he has hard core Communists.

The media have created the impression that Communism has been overthrown and a Communist world no longer exists. If this is true, there is no need for our mission. On the contrary, Communism has full power over a third of mankind, including China (1.1 billion), the USSR (280 million), Vietnam, Laos, Cuba, Ethiopia, Angola, and Zimbabwe. In Eastern Europe, Communist governments have been overthrown, but not Communist domination over the minds of men. Marxism has filled the whole populace with fear. People feared to say what they thought, whether by phone, in the marketplace, or even in the privacy of their own homes. Everyone was forced to inform on everyone else, even on members of their own family. Priests had to report privileged confessions to the police. Letters were censored. It was dangerous to meet a foreigner. Spies of the Secret Police were everywhere.

Publicly, everyone was on the side of the Communists, who always got 99% of the vote because no one dared to vote on his convictions. But in reality everyone hated the government. Millions have passed through jail. Many died before gaining freedom. Their relatives well knew what took place in prison. Torture has been used throughout the whole history of mankind. It would seem that all methods of torture were already known.

But Communists are innovators. Knowing that few men volunteer to do the work of torturing and those they victimize are many, thus allowing much respite between torture sessions, they forced others into torturing. Not satisfied with squeezing out of the victims a denial of their convictions and a betrayal of the secrets of their organization, the Communists tortured them to the extreme until they consented to become torturers of their brethren in faith. The result was that a new prisoner, thinking he was in a cell with fellow-believers, was subjected to the worst ignominies, not by officers of the Secret Police, but by those he had trusted and worshiped with. He was together with them day and night, tortured without pause, until he too consented to become a torturer. Some became sadists for life, others went mad.

All nations under Communism have been traumatized, not only those of Eastern Europe, but also Mozambique, Laos, Mongolia, etc. It will take decades for them to recover. The best medicine is the Gospel. The work of our mission in providing these people with the word of God is needed now more than ever before. Neglect of our duty angers God. Fulfilling it will make Him rejoice with singing. Jesus said, "Take heed that no one deceives you" (Matt. 24:4).

The warning is pertinent because Christians in the free world are in danger of being deceived by changes in the USSR. Apologists are saying, "Gorbachev is democratizing the country and extending liberty, so missions to the Communist world are no longer necessary." Lenin, founder of Communism and Gorbachev's avowed mentor, wrote: "Hundreds of epidemics and natural catastrophes are to be preferred to the slightest notion of God. Even flirting with a god is an unspeakable abomination." He also wrote: "The more representatives of the reactionary clergy are killed, the better." In their *Communist Manifesto*, Marx and Engels wrote that the aim of Communism is "the abolition of all religion and all morals." Gorbachev calls himself a Communist and remains such even if, like Yeltsin, he ceases to be a member of the Party.

Let us not forget that Communists seized power in Russia under the name "Social Democrat Party (Bolshevik)" and in Romania under the name "National Democratic Front." A change of name is not a change of heart. Stressing the point that Gorbachev is still a Communist and thus a God-hater, let us remember, too, that Castro, general secretary of the World Council of Churches, wrote in a letter to Gorbachev, "Christianity and Communism pursue the same aims."

Why So Much Suffering?

The one pain above all others endured by Romanians and inhabitants of other Communist countries is not knowing *why* they suffer such pain. The thought paralyzes the mind.

In the USSR, an estimated fifty million innocents were killed, another fifty million in China. No one knows how many were killed in Romania and other lands. One person was in prison for being a Jew, another for being an anti-Semite. Pastors were imprisoned for spreading religious propaganda, atheist lecturers for not having been effective in their anti-religious propaganda. Anti-Communists suffered next to convinced Communists who had fallen foul of their party about the interpretation of some tenet of Marxist teaching.

Communists used to condemn whole families if one member had done something amiss. I remember being imprisoned with a father and his four sons. His wife and daughters were in other cells.

Hungry and beaten prisoners renounced some of the few hours of sleep allotted them to discuss without end such questions as "Why did all this come upon us and upon the world?" "Is there a God?" "Where is God in all this? He is supposed to be all-powerful and loving. He could have kept these things from happening or could at least end them now. Why doesn't He?"

A Jewish prisoner went out of his mind. He constantly repeated one Hebrew word: *Maduah*— "why?" He said, "I could fill volumes with *mah* (what) is happening, but no one can reply to the question *moduah*."

I never met even one sufferer who was satisfied with the explanation that all evil—Auschwitz, the Gulag, Piteshti, and so on—is due in the last resort to the fact that Adam and Eve ate the forbidden fruit. Their sin was inherited by their descendants down all generations. It even passed into nature. Lambs are eaten by wolves, little fish by bigger fish, and children are beaten to the blood by Communist torturers in the presence of their parents to make them confess—all because many thousands of years ago a couple ate some fruit. The original sin is to blame.

It might be because of the sinful nature inherited from Adam that his descendants in our generation cannot comprehend this explanation. Other explanations I heard in these marathon discussions over the years were: "There is no God and therefore no sense." "It is punishment for our own personal sins." "Suffering is not real, it is *maya*. It belongs to a world of delusion." None satisfied.

One prisoner who had escaped from Nazi camps, in which he had lost almost his whole family, and now suffered under Communism, shouted in despair at a certain moment, "Haven't I endured enough from the Nazis and the Reds? Why must I bear the torment of listening to your senseless explanations? Suffering is bad enough. Don't make it worse with explanations." Believers who know God personally should trust him without asking questions. Our minds cannot comprehend the ultimate answers.

The Jewish people, generally considered to be very intelligent, had Jesus in the flesh in their midst. He spoke to them in plain language, but they did not understand Him even when He spoke in very simple parables. The disciples themselves understood Him only in part, but they believed in the unintelligible Jesus. This is faith. It supplements reason, which can know only an infinitely small range of things in this huge universe. We still don't know what an atom is. The image of an atom provided by science changes every couple of years. How then can we understand God?

I learned something in this regard from my grandson Alex when he was eight. We had guests in our home who discussed higher mathematics in his presence. I did not know how to hint to them in a polite manner that they should change the subject because it was boring for a child. So I asked him, "Alex, do you understand what we're talking about? Do you know what logarithms are?"

He replied, "Yes, I do."

Amazed, I asked, "What are they?"

"Logarithms are things I will learn about when I'm in high school."

Like children in school, Jesus' disciples advance

from the merely human to the divine. They are learners. One cannot learn in elementary school what is taught in universities. One day "I shall know even as also I am known" (1 Cor. 13:12).

Of all the explanations in answer to the question, "Why so much suffering?" the most compelling is simply, "We don't know." One day God will be all in all, which means that He will be all in Richard Wurmbrand. There will be no questioner, no questioned, and no question. We will be one spirit. It will be a mini-incarnation.

Jesus said, "To him who overcomes I will grant to sit with me on my throne, even as I also overcame and sat down with my Father on his throne" (Rev. 3:21). Somewhere there is a throne from which universes are created and ruled. This will be my throne too. Today I have to learn patiently all I will need at the moment of enthronement. The knowledge of suffering is part of the curriculum. Jesus himself was made perfect through suffering.

Some theologians adopt a softer tone than the Bible, claiming that God only permits evil. But according to Isaiah, God said, "I make the good and create the evil" (Isa. 45:7, as the original).

A racehorse trainer not only constructs a course but also obstacles which the horse must overcome. This comparison may seem inadequate to us because we have to overcome terrible physical and psychological torture. When we meet Jesus at last, we will see that our sufferings were insignificant in comparison with what we have attained. Scars will be ornaments. The wounded will be enriched by what they lost. Those who were killed will have exuberant life.

Christians face not the *problem* of evil, but its *challenge*. Problems depress, challenges spur us to activity. Christians in Romania see no possibility of solving problems, but they have learned to transcend them, to view them from heavenly places. For us, it was enough that the Communists tortured us. We decided not to add self-inflicted torments, such as philosophizing about the unknowable. Every torment was only a challenge to surmount the biggest obstacle: to win the tormentor through love.

David was our example. He wrote Psalm 9 on the tragic death of one of his sons, as is indicated in the title. But he does not complain about God and his own fate. He says what he would have said at the birth of a son: "I will praise you, O Lord, with my whole heart."

The Bible tells us that in the beginning was *Tohuwabohn*—dark, formless chaos. God, the Spirit of love, worked on this, encountering resistance to create a kingdom of unspeakable beauty and truth. I adore the audacity of this enterprise, His persistence in the face of failure, and His readiness to sacrifice His dearest for the salvation of the children of chaos. Psalm 121 tells us that from Him comes your help, not your sorrow.

The Legend of Kishagotami

In my visit to Romania, whenever I was confronted with questions about suffering, which were very often overwhelming, I told the old legend of Kishagotami, a young woman whose only baby had died and who could not bear to bury him. She went from one person to another asking how she could have him back alive.

One man told her, "Your only hope is the Savior. He has miraculous power like none other."

She brought her baby's body, knelt before the Lord, and begged. "Please resuscitate my child."

He replied, "Gladly, if only you will bring a little bit of salt to me."

Now, salt could easily be obtained, so she started to run. But he shouted after her. "The salt must be from a house in which no one has died."

"All right, all right!" she shouted back.

At every gate at which she knocked, she was gladly given salt. But when she asked if there had been a death in the family, she was always told, "I'm sorry, yes. My Father . . . or my spouse . . . or my child died."

She wept with everyone who gave such a reply, because now she knew what the sorrow of bereavement was. She comforted them and received comfort from the consolation she gave to others.

In the end she came to the Savior again and said, "Thank you for what you taught me. I will give back the body of my baby to the earth. Praise to you who give to my child and to all of us eternal life."

I have seen many a sad face illuminated when they heard Jesus' teaching.

"Why suffering?" is a wrong question. No right answer exists for wrong questions. Who can tell the melody of a peach? The question is wrong. Ask instead, "What good can I do with my sorrow? How can I use it to become more loving and more understanding towards others?" Sympathy will surely do them more good than theological explanations.

As for the rest, accept what Jesus said to Peter:

"What I am doing you do not understand now, but you will know after this."

Why Is There Cruelty in the Bible?

One more very troublesome question I often met in Romania was, "Why does God order so many horrors? He commanded Moses, Joshua, and others to exterminate whole populations, specifying each time that children and infants should be slaughtered, animals hamstrung, and trees felled. Such destruction surpasses even what Stalin and Ceaushescu have done."

I had heard these questions in the West, too, but rarely and not with such insistence as in my homeland. The many mass murders to which my nation was subjected made hearts more sensitive to such passages of Scripture. I am therefore against what is much practiced in the East nowadays: the indiscriminate distribution of Bibles to everyone we can reach. This was not originally God's intention. He gave to mankind a Bible and a church with wise teachers to explain it. Where there are no such teachers, it is preferable to give at first books explaining the main biblical messages.

But as I had to answer this difficult question, I preferred to give the simplest answer possible. In a sense, criminals decide what weapons the forces of law and order should use against them. Police don't use guns against pickpockets, because pickpockets have no guns. But they do use guns against armed robbers. Some methods used in just war might be considered inhumane if the same results could have been obtained otherwise. Against Nazi and Japanese aggressors who had tanks and bombers, tanks and bombers had to be used; otherwise evil would have been victorious.

God can evaluate evil in certain nations and social structures as we cannot. If widespread anti-American feelings in the West had not impeded the victory of the US in Vietnam, Cambodia would not have become Communistic and its leader Pol Pot would not have killed two million innocents. God alone knows the whole of a person, including the genes that will determine a baby's character. Jesus says about some, "It would have been better if they had not been born." He calls others devils and has a right to treat them as devils deserve to be treated. His decisions and actions are not subject to our judgment. We have to submit to His.

Lenin, founder of Russian Communism, said, "If Kerensky (prime minister of Russia before the Communist takeover) had arrested in time two dozen leaders of our party, we would never have come to power." And millions of innocents would not have been killed and mankind would have been spared a seventy-year bloodbath. No doubt some crusader for human rights would then have criticized Kerensky for depriving Communists of their "right" to prepare evil.

Don't philosophize about the Bible, but enter into the holy nation of God's children. Flee from those who deserve God's wrath. But do be attentive. In the original text of the Bible, there are no punctuation marks. There is not one single full-stop or comma. Only in translations is there a full-stop after expressions such as "They killed" or "God killed." In Hebrew, it is "The Lord kills and makes alive" (1 Sam. 2:6).

In heaven, we will meet many of those we thought were slaughtered. Alive and happy, they are thankful to God for elevating them from the level of pagan notions to that of children of God.

It is also good to know what the words "God said" mean in the Bible.

No one has seen the heavenly Father (except Moses, in one instance). When biblical authors, like today's believers, say, "God spoke to me," they mean an inner voice. We are composed of many parts. We have the conscious, the unconscious, different inclinations and impulses, even contradictory ones. All these can take, in our mind, the shape of voices that counsel and prompt us to action. Religious people call the voice that calls them to what they consider the noblest action the "voice of God." Sometimes they are right. But they can also be terribly mistaken. Ayatollah Khomeini, the Rev. Moon, Joseph Smith, founder of Mormonism—each was sure that what he said was "God's word."

Jesus is skeptical about some events in the Old Testament. The prophet Elijah caused fire to fall on the troop of a wicked king. Elijah was sure that his action fulfilled God's will. But when Jesus' disciples wanted to proceed in such a manner against those who opposed Him, confident that what Elijah had done was inspired by God, He chided them: "You don't know what manner of spirit you are of." The Old Testament prophets did not always act from the inspiration of God's spirit, though they believed they were.

Let us cherish Jesus' revelation: God is love.

The Task of Healing Nations

Communism is finished as a political institution

in almost all of the former satellite states of the USSR. But in Romania and Bulgaria, Communism still struggles to retain political power. Although it still does much harm, we can be sure that it is a rearguard fight; it is the despairing fight of a defeated enemy, the last writhing of a serpent before it dies. It will not survive in the Soviet Union either, except that Communism is more than a political institution. A Filipino who heard me speak twenty years ago in the Military Academy of Manila and who took part in armed fighting against Marxist guerrillas, reminded me that I said then something that made a lasting, because unexpected, impression on him: "There is a Communist rebel in each of us."

Marxist hatred of God is the most powerful expression of the human heart alienated from the Creator. It has always existed in fallen mankind in a latent form, but all societies tried to repress it. Communism lifted the lid. Marx wrote, "It is the evil side that makes history." I heard a Communist torturer say, "I thank God, in whose existence I don't believe, for making me live just at such a time when I can do all the evil I want without fear of punishment—yes, even with the assurance I'll be rewarded for it." This evil spirit has come out of the box under Communism, and the church will have to fight for many decades against Communism's poison in human hearts: hatred, envy, betrayal, lawlessness. (The Hebrew word *Belial* means etymologically "without yoke.")

In Romania, as in Bulgaria and Mongolia, the 1990 elections were free. After forty-five years of fierce terror, the Communists won great victories.

There were several serious reasons for this, which I have already mentioned. The opposition parties pleaded for friendship with the West. Romanians had been taught for decades that western governments were oppressors and exploiters and that their people went hungry. But the principal reason for the success of Communism lay elsewhere: who dared vote against the Party?

If Communism had fallen from power and the volumes of the Secret Police were opened, whole families would have been split apart because wives had denounced husbands; brides, bridegrooms; children, their parents; pastors and priests, members of their churches and vice versa. Even where the transition from Communism to a free society has been greatest, as in East Germany and Czechoslovakia, the archives of the Secret Police were not made public. If they were opened up to public scrutiny in Russia or Romania, these would cease to exist as nations. People would not be able to look into each other's eyes.

The pastor of a small Romanian Baptist church of only forty members confessed to me that he had been an informer of the Secret Police and that he knew five members who informed against him. I was in jail with an atheist who had had a quarrel with his bride. She told the police that he had expressed anti-Communist sentiments to her, and he received twenty years in prison.

Romania feels guilty. (In Nazi-occupied countries, there were also a significant number of collaborators, but the numbers were not so high as in Communist countries as the time-span was shorter.) Romania fears disclosure. Thousands voted for the

Communists they hated because they had been their accomplices. It is estimated that every tenth adult was an informer for at least a time. Our Orthodox synod called back Patriarch Theoctist, a bootlicker of Ceaushescu, when he retired after Ceaushescu's fall. The guilt had been collective, involving the priesthood as a whole.

When the final judgment is near, Satan will be released from his prison of a thousand years. Only he, restored to power, could cover up—men will hope—all the satanic deeds they themselves have done (Rev. 20:7).

All Romanian writers, almost without exception, had flattered Ceaushescu's pride, calling him "the greatest genius ever" and other such stupidities. Not one has admitted guilt. They all keep silent. The Romanian churches have an enormous task: to heal the nation.

God's Remnant

God has a remnant in Romania as He has in other Eastern European countries. Very many Christians died in the revolution of December 1989. Thanks to them, Ceaushescu has been overthrown. It was on Christmas Eve—a sign from God. The celebration of Christmas had been forbidden. But thousands of others are alive, and they have an amazing Christian spirit.

On the 13th of July, 1990, just a few days after so-called miners (in fact men of the former Communist Secret Police) had killed five, wounded hundreds, and arrested over one thousand peaceful demonstrators in Bucharest, there was another demonstration. Thousands marched with flowers in their hands, chanting a slogan that rhymes in Romanian: "You came to us with clubs and axes, but we come to you with flowers." The army sent out to quell the demonstrators was showered with flowers. The soldiers were overwhelmed. This time there were no bloody incidents. This was the first demonstration in which flowers were used against an oppressor, epitomizing Jesus' teaching: "Respond to evil with good."

Our mission had taught Romanians this for over twenty years through the written word and by radio. It was my message from the first day of my pastorate, at liberty and in jail, and it was what I preached in Romania on my return. It was Christ's triumph, but also the greatest personal satisfaction of my life.

And it has not remained the only one. The river Prut separates Romania as it is today from its province of Bessarabia, stolen by the Soviets and renamed the Moldavian Republic. On the fortieth anniversary of this tragic event, Romanians from both sides of the river turned it into a flowery carpet in a huge demonstration as people threw blossoms into the water. A people that has such a remnant will not perish. God will turn its mourning into feasting. Marx and Lenin, the deceivers, will be defeated by Jesus, the Truth.

But the true Romanian church, like that of other former Communist countries, needs your help. Give them Bibles and Christian literature. Give them Christian teaching by radio. Help the impoverished churches rebuild their prayer houses. Help former prisoners remake their lives. And help us bring Communists to Christ. If conquerors are not capable of converting the conquered, the conquests are not complete. The Allies conquered Germany in the First World War but did not convert the Germans to their ways of thinking. And so the stage was set for the Second World War.

Communists have lost decisive battles in Eastern Europe. If they are not won for Christ or at least for decent human behavior, the devil will be loose again in a very few years. We have to be on the alert. I certainly am. Many aged people live only on rehashing the past, which is nonproductive. I am only eighty-two. I still have a present as Christ's soldier and a great future in prospect. Come, fight with me.

About Richard Wurmbrand

In October of 1967, Pastor Richard Wurmbrand, along with his wife Sabina, founded a non-profit missionary organization to bring assistance to persecuted Christians around the world.

Today The Voice of the Martyrs, Inc., directed by Pastor Wurmbrand, continues to carry out this work. For more information about the mission activities or a complete listing of books and tapes by Richard Wurmbrand, please write to THE VOICE OF THE MARTYRS at the address below:

USA:	P.O. Box 443 Bartlesville, OK 74005-0443
CANADA:	P.O. Box 117 Port Credit Mississuaga, Ontario L5G 4L5
AUSTRALIA:	P.O. Box 598 Penrith NSW 2751
NEW ZEALAND:	P.O. Box 69-158 Glendene, Auckland 8
ENGLAND:	P.O. Box 19 Bromley, Kent, BR1 1DJ